# AMERICA & EUROPE

# AMERICA & EUROPE

*And other Essays*

BY

ALFRED ZIMMERN

*Essay Index Reprint Series*

## BOOKS FOR LIBRARIES PRESS
### FREEPORT, NEW YORK

First Published 1929
Reprinted 1969

STANDARD BOOK NUMBER:
8369-1117-2


LIBRARY OF CONGRESS CATALOG CARD NUMBER:
78-84350


PRINTED IN THE UNITED STATES OF AMERICA

# PREFACE

THE essays gathered together in this volume were written at various times and in various countries during recent years; but I hope that they will be found nevertheless to present an underlying unity of thought.

The paper which gives the volume its title is a very summary treatment of a subject which I am the first to admit requires far fuller exploration. The same is true of the essay comparing American and European university conditions. With the single exception of the economic and racial problems of the Pacific area, the contact between America and Europe constitutes the most important international problem of our time; and it is a problem which, in its deeper bearings, had hardly yet been realized, far less analysed and understood, on either side of the Atlantic. For us Europeans the United States of to-day is so new and strange an experience that it requires for its understanding something like a faculty for re-education; and such a re-education, even for those few who are willing to undertake it, is as slow a process as the development of America's discovery of herself, or, in other words, the working out of a distinctive American civilization.

The two processes must go side by side, at what pace and with what success in each case time alone can show. Meanwhile, until a fuller understanding is achieved, one can only place one's hope in the common sense and the shrewd and not unkindly tolerance which, despite their other diversities, remain common characteristics of the English-speaking peoples.

As regards the more strictly political essays there is a word to be added, since the Kellogg Pact, to which the reader will find an anticipatory reference on pages 197–198, has now been ratified by the United States and a number of other governments, and the leading states of the world are therefore now committed to the renunciation of war as an instrument of national policy in their relations with one another and to "the settlement or solution of all disputes or conflicts of whatever nature or of whatever origin they may be, which arise between them" by other means than force. At the moment of writing the peoples of Europe have practically no realization of the significance of this new international policy; that this should be so is but an illustration of the psychological conditions to which reference has been made in the preceding paragraph; the Pact was drawn up in the American fashion, and they do not understand what it means. But I am one of those who remain confident that events will soon conspire to reveal the practical consequences of the renunciation of the war instrument and thus to facilitate the development of all the various processes of international co-operation to which reference is made in these pages. A. Z.

Paris, March, 1929.

# CONTENTS

# I

## AMERICA AND EUROPE[1]

IN the summer of 1927, during the worst moments of
the franc crisis, a group of Americans assembling in a
sight-seeing car outside a tourist agency in Paris were
booed. This was cabled across the Atlantic as a news-item,
and the American press has been busy ever since discussing
whether Europe hates the United States and, if so, why.

As one whose work has for some years past taken him
to and fro between the United States, Great Britain, and
the Continent, I have been asked for a frank expression of
my opinion on European-American relations.

My view on the whole matter can be summarized in a
very few words. When the League of Nations project was
first being discussed in 1917, the late Mr. Jacob H. Schiff
was quoted as declaring: "Your League of Nations is not
enough: the root of the matter is economic." The last ten
years have made it clear to all of us, on both sides of the
Atlantic, that economic considerations underlie and
largely determine political happenings. To-day we are
being forced to realize that, if economics underlie politics,
there is a still more potent, if elusive, factor which under-
lies both the politics and the economics in European-
American relationships. That factor is the mind of the
dwellers on the two sides of the Atlantic. Varying the
phrase of Mr. Schiff, I would say to all those who are
grappling with the issues of the moment, whilst wishing
well to their efforts: "*Your economic solutions are not
enough: the root of the matter is intellectual.*"

[1]Contributed to the *American Review of Reviews*, March, 1927.

I

The real trouble between Europeans and Americans is simply misunderstanding—a misunderstanding so complete that its effects extend to every field of their mutual intercourse, political, economic, social and even philanthropic.

The relations between Europe and the United States will never be normal until this misunderstanding is removed. By that I do not mean to say that I look forward to the day when a majority of the inhabitants of the two continents will have an intimate understanding of the life and mind of the dwellers on the opposite side of the Atlantic. But I do look forward to the day when there will be a substantial number of individual Europeans and Americans who have won their way to that understanding. And especially I look forward to the time when the younger generation on each side is brought up to regard the Atlantic as an ocean interposed between equal continents and to look neither up nor down, but straight across the dividing water.

Relations between Europe and America have never been normal because they have never been equal. They have always been spoiled by some kind of unequal attitude, ranging all the way from the commands that emanated from the Old World under the old colonial system to the exhortations that emanate from the New World to-day. Whether it be the tie of political control, or of social prestige, or literary and artistic fashion, or of economic indebtedness, or of philanthropic obligation, the resulting situation is always, in essence, the same. Inequality begets embarrassment: and true friendship cannot grow up in an atmosphere of embarrassment.

As between Canada and Great Britain the problem has recently been solved, so far as it can be solved on paper, by the adoption of the formula of equal status. That formula and the spirit behind it need to be applied thoroughly and ruthlessly to every phase of European-American relationship until the last remaining cobwebs of a bad tradition have been swept out of every mind.

What is that bad tradition?

In the Old World it is the habit of regarding America as a vast and semi-barbarous extension of Europe. Blind to the real America, Europeans are prone to judge life in the United States by their own standards; and they naturally find much to criticize.

This habit has led to a vast deal of jocosity, some of it amusing, most of it merely ignorant foolishness, and nearly all of it an offense against international comity. If the League of Nations Committee on International Intellectual Co-operation were exercising its authority in Plato's Republic instead of in the easy-going world of to-day, it would issue a decree forbidding these literary gambols by over-smart Europeans and deporting contumacious offenders to another planet.

It is a real tragedy that the books about America which circulate most widely in Europe are generally so much overdrawn as to be totally misleading. They fall into three classes; there are the books of impressions which the European visitor to the United States, if he wields a pen, usually finds it impossible to resist writing; there are works of fiction, whether by Americans or with an American background; and finally there are the critical studies and satirical writings by Americans bent on improving conditions in their own country. The true works of interpretation that are being increasingly produced in these days are not known in Europe except in a very limited circle. Yet it is through such books, and the approach that they offer to the American scene, that Europeans can best learn to appreciate what is, and will always be for them, in the deepest sense of the word a New World.

This urge that drives the European visitor to write a book about his impressions is a healthy symptom, however inferior the resulting volume. It shows that the impact of America upon a live European mind spurs it to activity by contrast. America is for the European not simply another nation, as Italy is for a Frenchman or Denmark for a German: it is more even than another continent. It is a totally new experience. It is, I would almost say, an inoculation.

You can watch the European visitor and see how the infection "takes." In not a few cases, especially among hardened intellectuals, the organism is immunized against the germ. The effect of America in such cases is simply to make the subject more obstinately European. He reacts much in the same way as the Athenian intellectuals reacted against the vulgarian who came to preach to them a new way of life. Readers of Renan's *St. Paul* will remember the scathing passage in which he explains why St. Paul has left us no epistle to the Athenians. He could not found a church there because "the professor is the most difficult type of mind to convert." It is exactly the same kind of resistance that the European intellectual, secure in his own standards, offers to the impact of America. Because it grates on his sensibilities, he closes his mind and refuses to undertake the task of interpretation which is the justification of his existence.

This is the explanation of the strange caricatures and distortions of America which pass current from time to time in Europe. "Shylock" is the most recent and perhaps the most ridiculous of the whole series. Nobody who has had any real contact with America or with the American attitude toward money can imagine Uncle Sam in that rôle without smiling. Misers, usurers, and the like are the product of our own frugal and abstemious continent, with its traditional petty round of business, not of the land of boundless horizon and bounteous opportunity.

No wonder that Americans rub their eyes in surprise at seeing themselves as Europeans pretend to see them. The fact is, of course, that Europe does not really see them at all, for the simple reason that it is not looking at them. It is averting its gaze from them, and making up an imaginary picture from its own interpretation of certain trends of opinion and policy.

It would not be difficult to explain why practically all Europeans consider the policy of the United States Government mean, whilst many Americans consider it generous. But such an explanation would involve a survey of the course of political events in Europe and America since the Armistice, and would have nothing whatever to do with American miserliness, generosity or any other trait of the American character.

A simple illustration will make this clear. France is certainly more prone to produce the miser type than America, witness Molière's Harpagon, an unimaginable figure in American literature. Nevertheless if the United States were peopled mainly by Frenchmen, feeling as Frenchmen would naturally feel about the devastated regions, there is no doubt that American policy on the debt question would have been less miserly than it has been.

In other words, the accusation of miserliness which Europeans fling at America results, not from anything that we have observed in Americans, but from our own reactions toward a policy which has been actuated by entirely different motives. Since we are constitutionally unable, through our ignorance of American conditions, to understand what those motives are, we pick up the first brick-bat that comes handy for our ignorance and fling it in irritation across the Atlantic.

Nevertheless, in the world as it is to-day and as it is going to remain, to refuse to understand America is to exclude oneself, as the Athenian professors excluded themselves, from a vital and indeed indispensable experience. It is, in fact, to remain uneducated. We are only just beginning to consider what kind of education is needed for effective and harmonious participation in the new large-scale interdependent society of which we all now form part.

But, leaving that question for the time being on one side, let us turn from the conventional European distortions of America to the conventional American distortions of Europe.

In America the bad tradition takes the form of regarding Europe as a decadent continent. Blind to the living forces at work there, Americans judge Europe by their own standards and naturally they find much to criticize.

This European decadence appeals in different ways to different classes of Americans. In some, who have set their face toward America like Bunyan's pilgrim hastening from the City of Destruction, it inspires nothing but a confused memory of horror and disgust. For such, the "Old World," sunk in iniquity, is an eternal breeding place of war, tyranny, persecution and Machiavellian intrigue. They regard it in much the same way as Englishmen have for generations regarded the Balkans.

Minds like these—and they are numerous enough to have their representatives in high place—are hermetically sealed against good tidings from Europe. The progress of

the League of Nations, the Locarno agreements and other
signs of a new order in the Old World are not examined on
their merits but evoke the stereotyped response of cynical
incredulity: "Can anything good come out of Europe?"
I am reminded of a conversation I had at Geneva with
one of the League delegates from Abyssinia. I asked him
whether he believed that the League would ensure permanent peace. A sad expression came over his face as he
told me very definitely that he did not. When I asked him
why not, he replied in words which I shall never forget,
"We Abyssinians have noticed that you in Europe care
very much for wealth and power. So long as men care
much for wealth and power there will not be peace in the
world."

To such abstract reasoning there is no answer, except
perhaps to ask whether Abyssinians and Americans do not
themselves love wealth and power. The Abyssinian tradition about Europe is no doubt based on experiences that
are true, too true; so is the American. But they do not
help toward an intelligent understanding of the forces
that are working for better things! This kind of abstract
idealism is indeed one of the greatest obstacles that con-
front the true educator, not merely in the international
sphere but in every field of political affairs. Millions of
Americans are still seeing Europe as an abstract idea.

In other minds, hardly less absolute in their judgments,
the sad plight of decadent Europe evokes tenderer emotions. Millions of Americans are sorry for Europe. They
pity us. They feel compassion for our poverty, for our
backwardness, for the difficulties resulting from our unhappy divisions, for all the miserable consequences of our
past sins. They feel the urge of the good Samaritan. They
would like to bind up our wounds, assuage our hatred,

break down our barriers, promote our union. They see the City of Destruction not as an abomination to be avoided, but as the goal of an errand of mercy.

It is very hard for a European to write on this theme without seeming to be ungracious: but in a study of the intellectual relations between Europe and America it cannot be overlooked. For if the situation is not understood, American compassion may be even less helpful to European-American understanding than sheer aloofness and disgust.

Pity is an unequal relationship. Individuals do not like being pitied. Still less do nations. Still less does a whole continent. And if it is disagreeable to be pitied, it is particularly disagreeable to be an object of pity in quarters where one has been accustomed for generations to bestow one's own compassion.

My mind goes back, as I write, to an office in the capital of one of the Succession States of the Austro-Hungarian Monarchy in the first years after the Armistice. There sits an American in his shirt sleeves. His features, the broad brow and firm mouth and chin, recall the bust of a Roman emperor, as is not uncommon among big American executives, particularly in the Middle West. But he is not an emperor. He is Commissioner-General of Relief. And he is administering relief on the grand American scale, generous and far-reaching, but ruthlessly efficient. He has his charts, his card-catalogues, his survey results, his office force—in short, all the material instruments of American constructive idealism.

Before his eyes, outstretched on the wall, is a large map of the region within a part of which his operations extend, the line of the Danube cutting sharp through its midst. He has been discussing his problems, the unreasonableness of the natives, the difficulties arising from the languages, the customs barriers, the legacy of the war and the whole past history of the region. "Look at that river," he cried, striding to the map and drawing his finger along the Danube. "It is the Mississippi of Europe. It ought to be as free as the Mississippi from its source to its mouth. Then there would be a chance for these countries to enjoy some American prosperity. But they will never enjoy it," he went on, "till they have cleared away these ridiculous barriers, including all these outlandish tongues. Why can't they all talk a single language as we do? What is the use of all these languages of theirs? I would like to have a fortnight—just a single fortnight in their little Ministries of Foreign Affairs, and Ministries of Public Instruction. I would clear out their cobwebs." Thus, with a magnificent gesture, such as Julius Cæsar might have made in ancient Gaul or Britain, with their manifold tribes and kinglets, he swept away generations of history and tradition, of inherited culture and institutions.

He was an apostle of benevolence. But he was also, though he would be aghast at the title, an imperialist. And the imperialistic temper manifested in works of benevolence is no less unpopular than in its other forms. For benevolence is an unequal relationship and contains all the seeds of bitterness inherent in inequality.

It is this bitterness which is responsible for another of the legends about America which are very current just now in Europe, the legend of American hypocrisy. Americans of the Roman type that I have just described consider that they know better than Europeans themselves what is good for Europe. Their belief in their own solutions is perfectly honest and sincere. They have no doubt at all that the armaments, the tariff barriers, the languages and all the other complexities they come up against in European affairs are due to simple and easily removable causes. And they think they know how to remove them by the use of American influence which, reduced to concrete terms, means American money-power.

This has on occasion led American public men to feel it to be their duty to address Europe in language of mingled exhortation and menace, and to suggest visiting the whole continent or individual countries with pains and penalties if the exhortations addressed to them, purely for their own good, are not listened to. Europeans who read these addresses almost invariably regard them as hypocritical. Even Europeans who know America well find it difficult to resist the instinctive temptation to hurl the charge across the ocean and to couple it with a reference to the Eighteenth Amendment.

But Americans are not a nation of hypocrites any more than they are a nation of misers. Whether the Eighteenth Amendment has made Americans a nation of law-breakers it is not for an outsider to say. It has certainly not made them a nation of hypocrites. So far from pretending to be more virtuous or law-abiding than they are, they are apt to run to the opposite extreme and to let all the world know of their lapses from rectitude, whether in the unveiling of scandals in public affairs or in private conviviality. Here again the European, in his ignorance of American conditions, has invented a motive to explain a course of action that passes his understanding.

But there is another and more baffling element in the American tradition about Europe. Not all Americans either seek to avert their gaze from Europe or wish to reform her. There is a tradition of admiration.

American admiration of Europe, like American pity

and disgust, takes many and complex forms. It runs all the way from an understanding and assimilation of what is precious and permanent in European culture and achievement to blind and servile adulation. Toward the admiration of understanding, Europeans feel nothing but gratitude. It is an essential link in the chain of interdependence which unites educated men and women the world over. But the excesses of imitation and snobbishness which too frequently accompany the admiration of the unintelligent are every whit as disagreeable to Europeans as the opposite attitude of superiority. It constitutes another of those unequal relationships which prevent real understanding.

It is not healthy for Americans to regard culture as an exclusively European product, and it is certainly not healthy for Europeans to be regarded as a perfect model for American manners, American arts and American education. The process is demoralizing on both sides. The American who bows down blindly before European standards loses his American quality and receives a mere veneer in exchange; while the European who finds that his personality and surroundings have a power of attraction, or even a market value, simply because they embody elements of tradition, is subjected to an influence even more deadening. I remember one occasion on which this was first brought vividly before my mind. I was giving a lecture on America in an English University town, laying the emphasis, to the best of my ability, on the new contribution which Americans are making to the spiritual riches of the world. Suddenly I realized that I had before me an audience sharply divided into two parties. There were those who were glad to be given a clue to vital elements in the New World which had hitherto escaped them. But there was another section which, whether consciously or unconsciously, resented my account of an America which was losing its old colonial dependence on European standards and drawing its ability from native sources. Needless to say, it was, broadly speaking, the younger generation in the audience which constituted the former section, while the older portion constituted the latter. Thus it is that the old Europe seeks to enmesh America in the invisible filaments of its own decadence, whilst young Europe, sure of its own vital energy, responds to the sense of life on the other side of the Atlantic.

No, Europe is not decadent. Neither is America barbarous. Both continents are alive. Both are marching together toward a better future. But they have not yet learned to walk in step.

# II

## THE THINGS OF MARTHA AND THE THINGS OF MARY[1]

POLITICS were made for men and women, not men and women for politics. It is the realm of Mary, not that of Martha, which holds the master key to the happiness of mankind.

We shall realize this better after a brief survey of the nature and problems of these two contrasted realms. The contrast between them is as old as the dawn of self-consciousness, the revolt of the individual against the tyranny of the tribe or herd; and it was formulated, if not for the first time, at least in the most explicit and memorable shape, by the teacher who has done most of all men ever born to strengthen and deepen the sense of individuality, who came, in his own words, to give men life and to give it more abundantly. In teaching men to draw the distinction between their duty to Cæsar and their duty to God, as in the words he let fall amid the family at Bethany, and in his whole doctrine of the kingdom and his attitude toward the constituted authorities, Jesus set forth a view of the relation between personality and nationality, on the one hand, and political obligation, on the other, which, if it could once become the common property of mankind, would be the surest safeguard of peace: for it would remove the deepest and most passionate causes of difference from the political arena.

Wherein does the realm of Martha consist? What

[1]Contributed to the *Century Magazine*, New York, 1923.

exactly are "the things that are Cæsar's," with which statesmen and citizens are concerned? The best definition of the material of politics is the old Roman definition enshrined in our English word "republic." *Res publica*, the public thing, is that which is public or common to us all, the common basis of our separate existences. This common basis is, of course, an external and material basis. The common thing, or, as it may also be called, the public interest, is the outward order, the visible framework of society, what the Greeks called the equipment or dramatic appurtenances which enable us each to play our part in our individual lives. Without this common basis we should be units in anarchy; with it we are citizens, but not necessarily full-grown men and women. Politics is the art or business of adjusting these common affairs, and to be politically minded is to have a natural or acquired interest in this task of management or government.

During long periods of human history, especially during or after times of great social disturbance, or in times when the social equipment was being rapidly developed, the art of government has been generally regarded as the supreme art, and the perfection of external organization has been considered the chief and almost only test of civilization. The rulers of men, whether monarchs or statesmen, soldiers or civilians, have filled the history-books with their achievements and the market-places of cities and townships with their statues. Darwin, living quietly in a London suburb while he was revolutionizing the outlook of his generation, was almost abashed at receiving a visit from Gladstone, while it was Goethe the *Hofrat* of Weimar quite as much as Goethe the poet who preserved his self-respect while Napoleon was sweeping through his country.

But we of the twentieth century, brought sharply into contact with civilizations which have succeeded where ours have failed and failed where ours have succeeded, are beginning to alter our standard of valuation. We are beginning to realize that politics and government are only one side, if an important side, of the work of civilization; that they involve certain qualities and a certain training which are unevenly distributed throughout the world, unevenly distributed even through the civilized countries. It is perhaps in Russia, which we may call "backward" or "advanced" according to our predilections, that the old valuation of civilization in purely external terms is, on the surface at any rate, being most tenaciously adhered to.

Two peoples in the roll of history have shown conspicuous aptitude for government, the Romans and the English. Other nations, some of whom it would be invidious to mention, have been strikingly successful in what may be called pseudo-government; that is, in employing political means for other than political purposes, in using "the public thing" for private and personal ends. But "politics" in that sense of the term has nothing to do with government or politics proper: the corrupt politician is as different from a statesman as a medieval alchemist was from a chemist or as is the vender of a worthless drug from a conscientious physician, or a vaudeville performer from a great classical actor. Indeed, the vaudeville performer is pursuing a far more honourable calling than the politician, for he is frank and open in the acceptance of a second-class and imitative activity, while the politician is deceiving the people, and often himself as well, in reducing one of the most difficult and responsible of human activities into a competition in commercial bargaining and adroit intrigue.

What are the qualities which brought success to the Romans and the English in their work of government and enabled central Italy and southern Great Britain to become centres of great empires? Governor Hadley in his study of "Rome and the World To-day," has lately drawn attention to the remarkable similarity in physiognomy between the old Roman rulers and the American governing type of to-day; and there is no doubt that the work of organization carried on by Roman public men and their compeers in Great Britain and America has left its imprint in their faces. The distinctive qualities required for such work may perhaps be summarized in two characteristics, public spirit and judgment.

What we call "public spirit" is a moral quality, a particular and highly specialized form of unselfishness. It involves a concentration upon the public welfare of a zeal and a devotion which the non-political man, whether he be more intense or merely more sluggish in his attachments, prefers to bestow elsewhere. What we call "judgment," on the other hand, is an intellectual quality, a particular and highly specialized form of intellectual activity. It involves the power of taking a mass of facts, together constituting a "political situation," surveying them as a whole and framing a practical decision—a decision leading to action. To have a good judgment about a situation is not the same thing as to have an understanding of such a situation in all its bearings. Englishmen have not governed India by understanding her, nor did they quell the great Mutiny in 1857, which would assuredly have proved fatal to their rule had they been differently constituted, by their power of comprehending the motives which produced it. They held their ground by their power to comprehend not the underlying facts, but the urgent facts, and by their ability to decide as to "the next step." Just as public spirit, in its most concentrated form, involves a certain emotional abdication, so judgment, especially in an emergency, involves an intellectual abdication. The statesman, faced by the necessity of framing a practical decision, cannot afford to look too deeply into causes or to cultivate too nice a sense of intellectual consistency.

To sit on a committee is, for any one who has a keen intellectual life of his own, to suffer a species of martyrdom; in the process of arriving at a decision all the fine edges of the mind have to be rubbed off; or, if the victim resists, he earns the reputation of a bore who turns a business meeting into a philosophic dialogue, and seeks to apply to the world of mundane affairs, to drains and dispensaries and school management, the speculations that wiser men, who put things in their proper places, reserve for an evening discussion over the fragrance of a cigar.

The Roman and the Englishman both founded empires created by the genius of a single people and inspired, if not governed, from a single centre. But the age of empires is passing. The Empire of England has become, in designation and already in large part in fact, a multi-national "British commonwealth", and the other large-scale and heterogeneous dominions, the French, the Dutch, and, in its own distinctive way, the American, are grappling with similar problems. The true imperialist to-day is an internationalist. His scope can extend to nothing less than the whole planet. Augustus drew his frontier at the Rhine, and even twenty years ago Cecil Rhodes set limits to his statesman's vision; but the modern Cæsar, surveying the problems of the post-war world, must needs let his gaze travel round the globe. For while the qualities required of statesmen have remained unchanged, while public spirit and sound judgment are as indispensable to a Hoover and a Robert Cecil, to a Poincaré and a Mussolini, as they were to Augustus or the British makers of modern India, the nature of the material for which those qualities are required has changed beyond recognition. The industrial revolution and the consequent interdependence of the parts and peoples of mankind have changed the conditions of political activity. The problems of the modern world are no longer local, but large-scale, no longer concerned with the broils and prejudices of neighbours, but with forces which, in the vast sweep of their incidence, affect millions of men in all parts of the globe. We are only just beginning to realize that the age in which Alsace-Lorraine and the Irish question were first-class political problems has passed away beyond recall, and that in the new era which has dawned the distinctive problems which hold the keys of peace and war and command the daily vigilance of statesmen are of a different order.

Two or three of these may be indicated, if only to illustrate the type. No topic of discussion in the chancelleries contains so much material for controversy and possible warfare as that of the conservation of the world's mineral resources. Oil and tungsten, nickel and radium, involve no nationality problem. They are political, large-scale international material in the full sense of the words; and the statesmen who handle the practical issues of world-housekeeping—or, to put the words into Greek, "political economy"—arising out of them can do so without a trace, in their plans and policies, of national flavour. Here we are alone with Martha and her specialized tasks and technique.

The same is true of another great set of problems that is bound to assume increasing importance in the work of government—those relating to public health. Plague and cholera and syphilis, trachoma and malaria, know no national distinctions; there is no American health and English health, but only health; no Italian plague or Polish plague, but only plague; and as the problem is international, calling for uniformity in diagnosis, treatment, and preventive methods, so also must be the outlook and organization of the governing minds who deal with it.

A third and thornier instance is commercial policy. Much national passion and prejudice have gathered round tariffs, but trading, with all that pertains to it, is essentially an international profession, and the problems arising out of it, from the fraudulent dealings of individual merchants to the self-regarding policies of peoples, are becoming riper every day for treatment on an international scale: that is, by statesmen who can look beyond the local issues involved to the wider interests of the world as a whole. "The time may even come," writes one who is not an idealist, but a hardened official, "when no minister will frame a tariff affecting the trade of other countries without previous consultation with the countries which it affects, and without being prepared to defend it in Council with his colleagues of those countries and on grounds which he can justify before the whole world." [1]

The handling of these and similar problems must necessarily be keeping pace with the growth of the network of private contacts between country and country and continent and continent. The broad effect of modern statesmanship must inevitably be to bring about world unity, but a unity in the realm of Martha. When our modern Cæsars have taken the twentieth-century world, diagnosed

[1] *Allied Shipping Control* by Sir Arthur Salter, p. 280.

its ills, and provided appropriate treatment, when they have policed and doctored and made decent and habitable a world organized and knit together for plain people to live in with safety and comfort, they will have done no more than lay the foundation of a civilized world society. What remains—and it is the better half—is of the realm of Mary.

If the things of Martha are rooted in the common life of man in society, the "better things" that Mary cared for are rooted in the inner life of the human soul. And the chief characteristic of the human soul, what constitutes its humanity, is its individuality. No two trees, no two dogs or horses are alike, and still less are two human beings alike. This hoary platitude, with which stone-age man was already familiar, would not be worth repeating were it not constantly being ignored in practice. But in a society which "tests" human beings as though they were standard pieces of mechanism, which loves to create frames and pigeon-holes and then to fit its human material into them, which has constructed for the use of its citizens sets of orthodox trappings for use in this or that walk or groove of life and is indignant when men and women prefer to walk along God's highway of earthly existence in the gait and guise that pleases them, it is well worth while to emphasize the glory of human uniqueness.

If men and women cannot be made to a pattern, neither can nations. If diversity is the glory of human beings as human beings, it is also the glory of nations as nations. The greatest men that the world has seen were also the most completely individual, the most different from all other men. Jesus was a Jew, and every one who knows the Jewish soul can recognize the Jewish quality in his personality. But he achieved his supremacy not by remaining true to the Jewish type, but by being himself, by becoming himself. The same is true of all the greatest human figures. "What really interests me in Plato," a distinguished philosopher once told me, "is that part of his work for the understanding of which no knowledge of Greek civilization is required." The remark scandalized me at the time, entangled as I still was in excessive preoccupation with externalities; but now I understand that its paradox conceals an element of vital truth. True, my friend, who had been brought up on the classics, did not realize how his own knowledge of Greece enabled him to rise with Plato above the general Hellenic level to the philosophic altitudes above. You cannot think away something that you have never thought. Really to understand Plato, you must begin your journey by the olives of the Ilissus and among the inquisitive crowd of the Athenian market-place, and work steadily upward, past the shepherds' huts and the mountain pastures, till you emerge on the high peak, with its serene survey over land and sea. But the mountain itself, like the spirit of those who win their way thither, is far above the common life below. Plato is an Athenian transfigured; Shakespeare an Englishman, and yet more than an Englishman; Goethe a German, yet not a typical German; Dante an Italian, yet a miracle of human power and passion for all time. Their greatness is built up on their nationality and cannot be disjoined from it; but it is distinct and unique in itself. Of all the four it may indeed be said that every line that they have left us is pure autobiography. They had so completely individualized themselves that every outpouring of their spirit has the same personal note.

And the same, if in a lesser degree, is true of the achievement of nations. If Athens and Florence, England, France, and Flanders, have won international fame for the production of their national cultures, it is not because they strove to be national, to drill their people according to a standardized preconception of the time, but because they gave Athenians and Florentines, Englishmen, Frenchmen, and Flemings, the occasion and inspiration to be themselves. The nationality which we now admire in their work springs straight out of their personality, and it is this nationality which has made their work international and immortal. Devised according to an international pattern, it would have been lifeless; devised according to a national pattern, it would have remained on a common conventional level. Allowed to spring up out of the uniqueness of individual living and thinking, it has become a permanent power in the civilization of mankind. If America is disappointed with her national culture and its representatives, it is not to systems and programmes that she must look for her salvation.

Let us now set side by side and contrast the two kinds of forces or influences. On the one hand we have the realm of Martha, the world of politics or common affairs, a world of public spirit and efficiency, of organization and standardization, always tending to a larger and larger scale, and now becoming increasingly international. On the other we have the realm of Mary, the world of the individual human soul, a world personal and intimate, intense in its feelings and attachments, and capable of inspiring not the duty-bound activities of public spirit, but the all-pervading and integrating passion, alike unreasonable and unfathomable, which we call love.

If men realized the difference between these two realms and between the motives and impulses which operate within them, half the political problems of the world would be quickly solved. For most of these so-called "problems," including those which seem most hopeless and intractable, arise simply from an overlapping of the two realms and from a failure on each side to realize that the two parties are dwelling on different planes and speaking different languages. All strictly political problems are relatively easy to solve: they are simply problems in applied science, whether it be economics or medicine or engineering or political science in the narrower sense of the term. As Sidney Webb, that prince in the study of externalities, once remarked, "patriotism is simply a problem of administrative areas." If it were, if this were all that the statesman was concerned with in Ireland and India, in Haiti, Liberia, or east-central Europe, his task would be simple. Draw scientific frontiers, establish an efficient government within them, with or without a show of democracy, and man in his threefold character, as Mr. and Mrs. Webb see him, man the producer, man the consumer, and man the citizen and defender of his home, will be duly satisfied.

But, unfortunately, men and women are not fashioned on this simple threefold pattern, nor are they gifted, as a rule, with a power of analysis enabling them to distinguish between the various elements in their thought about nations and commonwealths. And it is just from this confused thinking, this entanglement between the common and the individual, between the outer and the inner, that the most obstinate political and national problems arise. The Irish question is a good example. In its essence it was a struggle between the advocates of the two different realms, between the English, the political people *par excellence*, who sought to "politicize" it, as against the Irish, for whom the mystical Ireland of the heart is so much nearer and more

real than the visible island, with its highways and rail-
roads, its creameries and fisheries, as an object of government. The English solution of the Irish question was to
kill Irish nationality with kindness; in other words, with
good government. To the Englishman, dwelling in the
realm of Martha, the break-up of the United Kingdom
seems, or seemed until he was harried out of his common-
sense habits, a crime against the uniformities which make
for prosperity and good government. "Was there ever
such lunacy proposed by anybody?" cried Mr. Lloyd
George at Carnarvon in October, 1920, in reference to the
details of a dominion home-rule scheme for Ireland; and
the solution which the same statesman later carried
through pushed the lunacy still further, because it par-
titioned the island and built up a customs barrier through
her green lands from sea to sea. To a British audience the
inconveniences of separate industrial legislation, separate
rates of taxation, a separate fiscal system, seemed un-
answerable arguments for the maintenance of the union.
But the Irishman, dwelling in another realm, never saw
these arguments, still less tried to meet them. For him it
was enough to know that the union, and the English
garrison, maintained in his beloved country an element
disturbing to his spiritual peace; and having decided to be
"free," and that inner freedom was dependent upon
certain external arrangements, he faced the practical consequences with unflinching patriotic faith, but without
the businesslike calculation of statesmanship. Now that
the Free State is in being, Irishmen in their turn are facing
the responsibilities of Martha, and when they heed the
scriptural injunction as to the duty to Cæsar and the duty
to God, they must sometimes ruefully reflect that the
wisest of all teachers left it to each group of his pupils, in

each particular case, to decide *how much* of duty and devotion should be apportioned to each sphere.

There is indeed only one solution of the Irish question, as of the many other questions in which the two realms overlap. It is to draw them asunder and set each on its proper plane. It is to *depoliticize* nationality and to *de-emotionalize* politics; to take nationality and its intimacies clean out of the world of state housekeeping and efficiency, and to rescue politics, in its turn, from the rhetoric and rhodomontade, the emotional suggestions and confusions which impede the exercise of the statesman's sober judgment and public spirit. When politics become reasonable, and when men become as responsible in the discussion of political issues as in dealing with their own practical private concerns, we can look forward to a world set free from the fear of war. But just so long as passion runs riot on public issues, whether it be the sentimentalism of the pacifist, the so-called loyalty of the patriot, or the sheer emotional debauchery of the demagogue, conflict will be an ever-present possibility. For emotions do not confer; they collide, and under the impact of a collision they are apt to turn into their opposites. How often have we seen the peace fanatic in one cause become the war fanatic in another! There is no room in politics for emotion unballasted by reason, and it is one of the peculiar dangers of modern democracy that it affords an avenue to cheap success for men who, discontented, maybe, in their own intimate life, seek emotional relief in impassioned appeals to mass prejudice. The affairs of the republic are not a narcotic or an anodyne, to be turned to in the stress of dissatisfaction and *malaise;* still less a spectacle or a pastime, a contest in which victory goes to the quickest wits or the readiest tongue.

Americans seem, to the outside observer at any rate, to be particularly susceptible to the temptation unduly to emotionalize their politics. American history originates from the victory of a political dogma which has now almost become an inherited mode of feeling, and thus reason seems to find less easy an entry into the world of American political discussion than in communities where an older tradition and a wider background afford more emotional outlets in other directions. But as America comes of age and as Americans grow into their environment and imprint their own intimate and integrated personality upon it, this difficulty will diminish; and it should not be long before the mood evoked by the Stars and Stripes becomes predominantly one not simply of buoyant enthusiasm and almost mystical reverence, but also of serious and meditative responsibility.

If the Irish question is an example of Mary impinging on the realm of Martha, there are other current controversies in which we can plainly watch the opposite process. A typical instance is that of the struggle for survival among languages. The tendency of the present-day world is to concentrate human intercourse more and more upon relatively few world media and to allow the large-scale forces of modern life to crush the less widely spoken languages, what are called in India the vernaculars, out of existence. Some have even gone so far as to construct new languages in the name of progress, tongues fit to be spoken by the *Robots* of "R. U. R." Yet every student of literature and every lover of human nature must realize that language is the magic casket of nationality and that a people which has lost or bartered away the tongue of its ancestors has surrendered with it a large part of its soul. Only the strongest peoples, such as the Scotch, can win their way to self-expression in an alien medium adapting it to their nature rather than being adapted by it.

Here, too, it is a question of how much is to be rendered to Cæsar. That all Welshmen and Irishmen should speak English is a necessary concession to Martha, but it is too often forgotten that bilingualism, the ability to speak two languages currently and fluently, is not an inconvenience, but an enrichment. Nor need the older ancestral language be relegated to Sunday and to sacred and traditional usages. No one who has ever seen a Welshman converse in English, and then, turning to a compatriot, unbutton his very soul, as it were, in his own tongue can doubt that the "vernaculars," so much despised by the practical man, have a rich future before them if men will but have the courage to be true to their deepest instincts. It is not for an outsider to make practical suggestions to American educationists on this subject, but he may be permitted to draw attention to the splendid and varied endowment of inherited cultures and qualities with which America has become enriched during the last century—an endowment which makes her the natural centre of internationalism and of the processes of mutual understanding between nations, and to deplore that so much of precious quality has been allowed to run to waste, and even to perish in contempt, through the ignorance and short-sightedness of sons of Martha in high places. But happily the exponents of the newer school have realized the harm that has been done, and are exerting themselves manfully to repair it.

A struggle of the same kind as that which we have observed in the life of society is being waged incessantly within the mind and spirit of the individual modern man and woman. On what principle is he to choose his mode of livelihood? Shall he aim at outward success or at inner satisfaction and harmony? And when he has chosen the better alternative and dedicated himself to an employment that is also truly a vocation, how far is he to carry his indifference to external standards and his sacrifice of worldly success? To what extent is he justified in allowing the form or quality of his work to be affected by the demand of the popular market? How many a potential poet and artist, philosopher, historian, and essayist, endowed with the ability to leave behind him first-rate and enduring work, has been tempted away by the sons of Martha into that modern city labyrinth where high purposes are diluted into trivial achievements, where the daily output of chatter with pen or pencil takes the place of the considered utterance to which men might have listened in after years! When we compare our unparalleled opportunities for first-rate achievement with the relative leanness of what the modern world has to show for its pretended efforts, we do not sufficiently reflect on the manifold ways in which ardent aspiration and budding genius are constantly being thwarted and stifled by the very mechanism which purports to exist for their service. How often has the cold indifference or wilful opposition of society led genius to suicide! And how much oftener to a life of concession and compromise, which, being a living extinction, is worse than the incident of death itself!

And yet the externalities remain, solid, inexorable, unavoidable, as real as the body itself, against the limitations of which our souls often chafe. Even the loyalest servant of the Muse, even the most absent-minded philosopher, must have his dinner and the wherewithal to procure it.

Even the community of anarchists, retiring from an over-regimented world to seek serenity in the backwoods, must have its humble highway and levy the rates for its upkeep. And Jesus himself, when he gently rebuked Martha for being "cumbered with much serving," neither condemned her activities nor refused to partake of their achievement. The practical decision, here as always in this world of sun and shadow, of body and soul, of urgent necessities and abiding eternities, involves a working adjustment between the forces and influences of the two realms. How is that adjustment to be made? That question each modern man and woman must decide for themselves. But two guiding considerations suggest themselves.

In the first place, we make our adjustment best when we make it consciously and deliberately. To flee from the modern world because it is full of machinery is to repeat the error of monasticism. Let us live boldly and freely in it, using what our environment has to offer us, but not allowing it to use us. The world about us is full of men and women who, like a globe-trotter's baggage, are continually being plastered afresh with new labels: every incident, every idea, every article and conversation, leaves its impact on the yielding surface of their nature. This is not to live, but simply, in the words of the poet, to be

> "Whirled round in earth's diurnal course,
> With rocks and stones and trees."

Others, seeking to be "practical," form a hard shell of resistance against outward influences and become assimilated, in their inner nature as in their daily habits, to the machine or organization which they are paid to serve. Either way lies suicide and the disintegration of personality. You cannot serve both God and Mammon: neither can you serve both the God within you and the machine without. To serve a machine is to become a machine.

Secondly, the aim of the adjustment must be to attain to unity, to a twofold unity, a unity in the outer realm as in the inner. No serious-minded modern man, however clamant the call of his inner life, can afford to dispense with the duties of citizenship or with the responsibilities of international adjustment. The task still remains before us of making this world a fit place to live in for the children of men. Invention and organization, both in natural science and in the arts of government, have shown us the possibilities which, for the first time in the planet's history, lie before us in this endeavour; and we dare not neglect them.

But to this outward unity of the statesman's dream there must be an inner unity to correspond. If we rest satisfied with the ideal of "a world set free for democracy," we may but have pointed the way to a world commonwealth fated, like imperial Rome, to perish of inward inanition. Leagues and commonwealths are made for man, not he for them. If Cæsar's affairs are ever to be set in true order, it will be because the generation which has done its duty by them has also done its duty to God; because there is at last a world of men and women who are masters both of their destiny and their environment, who have learned how best to employ the many treasures of their personal and national inheritance, to draw all that is best and finest in the world about them into the broad, flowing stream of a personal life and a national culture, and to say with renewed thankfulness every day, as they survey the diversity of human gifts and obligations, "O Lord, how manifold are thy works! in wisdom hast thou made them all."

# III

## AMERICAN UNIVERSITIES[1]

As I look back over two years spent chiefly in American universities, one impression stands out above all others and will surely remain a permanent memory. It is the golden quality of the American undergraduate. I have had close contact with students in many countries—in England, in Wales, and on the Continent of Europe—but it has never been my good fortune to encounter pupils who, with negligible exceptions, were so alert and receptive, so friendly in the give and take of the mind, so loyal, so understanding, and so warmly appreciative of care bestowed upon their intellectual needs.

The American student takes a little knowing, and in these days, when every visitor from overseas is supposed to come armed with propaganda, he quite rightly begins by being on his guard. But, once his suspicions are broken down and his natural independence and initiative attracted, he takes to his work with zest and makes astonishingly rapid progress. When I compared the results of the written work and discussions at Cornell in May with those of the preceding October I could only say that, in Oxford, it would have taken two or three years to effect a similar improvement.

This judgment, I know, will surprise the pessimists, who tell us that the American university is filled with pleasant-mannered young men, who care nothing for the things of the mind and are bent only on getting through the

[1]Contributed to the Educational Supplement of the *New York Evening Post*, 1923.

31

minimum requirements with the least amount of trouble for themselves. But I would ask the pessimist whether he has ever really tried to know the objects of this indiscriminate criticism. You cannot interest the American student, or any student, in the things of the mind unless you teach him. And by teaching I mean real teaching, the kind of teaching that Socrates gave, not the recital of lecture notes to a large dumb crowd in an imposing hall, nor a "quiz," designed rather to find out what "assigned readings" they have failed to absorb than to discover the real drift of their natural interest in the subject.

"How can a man learn from one who is not his friend?" said the Greek philosopher long ago.

Mr. Albert Mansbridge placed these words on the title page of the book in which he described the remarkable success of the English Workers' Educational Association in bringing university teachers into contact with working men. Exactly the same is true of teaching within the walls of the university. Make your classes small enough to enable you to know your students and for them to know you, and you can create an atmosphere of friendly discussion in which ideas can germinate and flourish. Keep your classes large and they will remain dumb driven cattle, apparently quite innocent of intellectual desires and motions. But don't imagine that this stolid exterior represents the reality of young college-bred America.

"It must be hard work?" Of course it is. Everything worth while is hard work. If you don't want to work hard, don't be a university teacher. And it is harder work in America than in England because of the pressure of numbers. As an Oxford tutor I used to give two lectures a week and take some fifteen students individually. At Cornell, I gave two lectures a week and took eighty students in the first term and 140 in the second, not, indeed, individually, but in groups averaging a dozen each—small enough, that is, for each student to feel himself to be a real person and not a cipher and to be called upon once at least in the term to take the leading part in the discussion. To take personal contact with 140 students a week is no doubt an exacting task, and I should add that I could never have undertaken it without the collaboration of my wife. But the result, not merely in the joy of achieved results, but in insight into the problems of the coming generation, far more than repays the effort.

One thing that strikes me, as I go over the faces at Cornell in memory and compare them with my Oxford students, is their heterogeneity. It is often said, especially by those who know America only from Europe, that Americans are standardized and all of a type. Nothing could be less true of young America, as I have seen it at Cornell and elsewhere. The Oxford undergraduate is far more homogeneous in outlook, manners, opinions, experiences, and ambitions than the Cornell undergraduate. This is but natural, since the Oxford undergraduate is drawn predominantly from a single social class in the stable society of a small island, while Cornell students are drawn from the length and breadth of a vast and rapidly changing continent and from homes representing every variety of heredity and social circumstance. Thus, to know Oxford is not to know England, although it is a liberal education in English history, while to have taught in an institution like Cornell is to have an insight into American life, from the metropolis to the farm, and from the bank and department store to the small town business, together with a liberal education in the geography, not of the United States only, but of Canada and the Caribbean.

Another characteristic that has impressed me in my contact with American students is that it is easier than in Europe to relate their knowledge to life. The British University student has generally but a limited background of practical experience. He may come, as most Oxford and Cambridge students do, from a comfortable middle-class home and be provided with an ample allowance, or he may have made his way to college through scholarship and parental sacrifice, and from one of the new state-aided high schools. But in neither case is he likely to be spending his summer vacation on a farm or behind a counter; still less will he be able to "work his way through," while he is actually in residence at college.

It is one of the glories of the American university that it is not yet the home of a leisured class: and the fact that, at Cornell for instance, the overwhelming proportion of the students support themselves by their own labours during the summer, instead of climbing in Switzerland or shooting grouse on their fathers' moors, is of distinct intellectual advantage. The American student has a fund of living experience, which the teacher, endeavouring to relate book knowledge to life, can always be sure of being able to turn to account. Over and over again during the class work at Cornell my mind has harked back, not to the lively, scintillating, but often over-sophisticated conversation of Oxford, but to broader, simpler and manlier discussions, to which I listened nightly at the time when my work lay in the adult education movement.

The American student may know less than the Englishman; his mind may be less nimble, his reading less extensive, his reasoning less facile, his prejudices more on the surface; but he has the inestimable advantage of being more grown up. All he needs is for his intellect to catch up with the rest of him.

The new teacher in an American University is naturally surprised at first to discover the degree to which these practical preoccupations seem to overshadow the intellectual scene. "Activities" of one sort or another, whether it be managing baseball, financing a magazine, or organizing the editing of an annual, seem to claim pride of place over mere reading and thinking. But, if he is wise, he soon learns not to exalt the latter at the expense of the former, but to attempt to relate the two. That "activity" with which the American student is bubbling over, so that he dispenses it with a liberal hand on everything that comes his way, is the precious material of the university teacher's art. All that is needed is to guide and channel it. Some of the best work of my year in Cornell was done by athletes who had discovered how to transpose into another field the mental energy and concentration called out in them in their sports. There is a football coach at Cornell from whom some of the members of his team have learned much more than football.

This suggests a deeper consideration, which I can only touch on briefly here. It is that the nature of American life and the course of American development affect the scope of the teacher's art in ways which, as it seems to me, have not been sufficiently recognized by American educators. If the object of education is to enable men and women to understand, in the fullest and deepest sense, the world they live in, or, to use a definition of which I am rather fond, to harmonize the outer world with the inner, then surely the American teacher must be careful, in the selection of the materials of "culture," to keep as close as he can to the first hand experience of his pupils. A great deal of the current aversion to what is "high brow" is simply a healthy reaction against the second-hand. The great difficulty in handling what are called "arts subjects" in America is that they are to so large an extent European.

Let me hasten to make clear, lest I class myself with the Philistines, that I am not saying that young Americans should not read the Funeral Speech of Pericles, because it was written on the other side of the Atlantic. I am only saying that the problem of presenting it to him in a living way, in a way that will appeal to his own inner and outer experience, is the major problem of American arts education, and that until this is recognized the engineer, the chemist, the geographer, and even the teacher of journalism and public speaking will have a natural advantage over those who deal in the old classical wares, be they Greek or Latin, English, French, or German. For the natural sciences, at any rate, do give a discipline, narrow and specialized though it may be, while the student who has taken a group of cultural courses too often emerges with nothing more than a mass of unrelated knowledge and some pretty accomplishments which, in his heart of hearts, he may consider more suitable for his sister than for himself.

The conclusion to be drawn from this is not that the American student, even when his bent is towards the arts, should receive his early discipline and training in the sciences, but that he needs more skilful and careful teaching in the arts than his European compeer. The university problem is everywhere primarily a problem of teaching; but nowhere is this so pre-eminently so as in America.

I had not been long at Cornell before I made two observations. One was that whereas at Oxford teachers have "studies" in which to receive their students—pleasant living-rooms lined with bookshelves and furnished with armchairs and tables covered with recent books and reviews—in America teachers have "offices"—"Room 321,

sixth door to the left on the third floor of the Arts Build-
ing"—and not always very much like an abode of the
Muses when you get there. My second observation was that
practically none of my students looked upon university
teaching as a desirable career for themselves or their friends.

On reflection I realized that these two phenomena were
closely related. The great difference between British and
American university administration is that in England
universities are controlled by scholars along lines of administration which, however much open to criticism in
detail, have been evolved to meet the special needs of institutions of learning, whereas in America universities are,
on the whole, administered by business men along lines
which are assimilated, as closely as the differences of function and circumstance permit, to the organization of a
business enterprise. And as, in the nature of the case, the
assimilation cannot be complete, there is necessarily something unsatisfactory about American university organization which affects the prestige of a university career in all
sorts of subtle ways. Young Americans, who are very sensitive in their appreciation of values, feel that if they are
to go into business they would rather take contact with
the real thing and not with its pale academic imitation.
The natural-born scholar, on the other hand, feels himself
irked and incommoded in a hundred little ways by the prevalence of types of organization and standards of judgment
which he feels to be wholly out of place in an institution of
higher learning.

American university administration has lately been
under fire from many quarters. I do not wish to express an
opinion on the merits of the controversy between the
trustees of a well-known New England college and its distinguished president, with whom I enjoyed the delights of

intellectual combat in his stimulating classroom some eighteen months ago. Still less do I wish to associate myself with the sweeping accusations and insinuations brought by Mr. Upton Sinclair against the whole tribe of trustees and university governors. I have had the pleasure of meeting a number of university trustees on different occasions and have found them to be what I should have expected, sincere, straight-forward, fair-minded, public-spirited men, unfeignedly anxious to do their best for the institution under their charge.

Nevertheless the fact remains that the business man put in charge of an institution of higher learning is undeniably in a false position. His training and outlook inevitably drive him to apply forms of thinking and to favour policies which, however sagacious in business, are wholly unsuitable to education; and the greater his sense of responsibility and his anxiety to make a success of his trusteeship, the more calamitous are his policies likely to be. A business man is no more competent to run a university than a scholar to run a bank or a factory. The business man is trained to look for "efficiency," for a smooth-working organization, for definite and measurable results, for a valuable and imposing plant, for the outward and visible signs of "success." The scholar, who knows that his standards are not the standards of the crowd, is concerned not with quantity but with quality, not with the mounting curves of statistics but with the spirit working in secret places, not with the piling up of buildings but with the transmission of living ideas. No doubt universities, like churches, need buildings and equipment and can not dispense with the services of the sons of Martha skilled in these matters. But business ability should surely be kept, as it is at Oxford, in its natural place, which is

that of advising rather than controlling the directors of
university life and policy.

The first encounter which stands on record between
scholarship and Big Business was the famous interview
between Solon and Crœsus. On that occasion the sage
assumed a distinct position of moral superiority, and his
European successors have on the whole maintained this
position ever since. It is to this, to the respect felt by the
leaders of the outside community for the disinterested pursuit of knowledge that the prestige and attractiveness of
academic life in Europe have been due. No one had set
forth the ideal of the scholar's life more eloquently and
persuasively than Emerson in his Phi Beta Kappa address
on the American Scholar. But the eighty years and more
which have since elapsed do not yet seem to have made
scholarship truly at home in the American university.

Perhaps the best evidence of this is the position of the
American college president. Nothing seems more surpris-
ing to a European sojourning in an American college community than its leadership. In England the Vice-Chan-
cellor, or the Warden, President, or Master of a college is
a teacher who has won authority enough among his fellow-
teachers to be able to preside over them, to harmonize
their activities, and to promote among them a living sense
of the unity of knowledge and of the true purposes of a
university. I do not say that presidents of this type do not
exist in America: I have indeed met one or two both in the
East and in the West. But they are the exception, not the
rule. The typical university president, whatever his
scholarly attainments in the past, seems to have drifted
into the position of being the travelling salesman of a
body of business trustees, or, in the case of State institutions, the lobbyist skilled in the defence of the interests of

his enterprise. Ready to pack his bag and dash into his sleeper at an hour's notice, he spends his time at conferences, at alumni banquets, at the celebrations of allied institutions—anywhere but in his own library and among his own faculty and students. In more than one institution, after waiting to see the great man after his return to his alma mater from a business journey, I found him so overwhelmed with fatigue that he could hardly keep his eyes open.

Meanwhile the university itself languishes for lack of leadership. The head of an Oxford College is personally acquainted, as a matter of course, not only with his faculty, but with all the inmates of the college. The head of an English university knows all his faculty and a considerable proportion of his students. American universities are often so stupefyingly large that the president would, in any case, find it difficult to know even his professorial staff; but his outside duties almost inevitably make it impossible. I once happened to be present when the president of a State university was receiving three of his deans to report on the progress of their work during his absence. It was evident from the conversation that their relations were not those of a working head taking contact with his lieutenants, but rather those of an august being from outside, resembling the "visitor" of an Oxford college, being informed of the main lines of work with which he was not expected to be familiar in detail. Under such circumstances, human nature being what it is, it is inevitable that the president should only be told what it is good for him to know, and that the power should gradually devolve into the hands of the departmental chiefs. And the natural result of this is to break up the university—the old mediæval *universitas* of knowledge—into a number of practically autonomous departments or even, as they are sometimes called, colleges. The natural link between the arts and the sciences is broken down, and even in the arts themselves, classics, English literature, the Romance languages, history, political science, and economics, all members of the noble family of the humanities, each sets up house for itself and tends to build it so large as to leave little occasion to take contact with its neighbours.

This fissiparous and disintegrating process has been reinforced by the prevalence in American universities of intellectual specialization of an extreme and ultra-German type. For the minute and special studies carried on by young scholars in German and other Continental universities under the direction of great masters like a Mommsen and a Harnack there is something to be said. But the transplantation of this method from German to American soil and the attempt to apply to the energetic independent-minded American a system that succeeded, alas, only too well, with the industrious, obedient German has been an unmixed calamity. It would be a source for Homeric laughter if it were not a real tragedy, to watch red-blooded young Americans of pioneer stock, who ought, by every law of their nature, to be adventuring gayly and boisterously into the vast and alluring *terra incognita* of humane learning and ideas, pinned down by a Prussianized preceptor to a year's research for a master's degree, to be followed by two years more for a doctor's, on the ablative absolute in Cicero or the House of Lords during the reign of Edward V. The increasing vogue ("popularity" would be too grimly unsuitable a word to employ) of these higher degrees constitutes a very real deterrent to the would-be American university teacher. A country in which, as I am assured, a brilliant scholar and live teacher cannot reckon on getting a good university appointment unless he has first blunted his edge and narrowed his outlook and interests by a course of soul-destroying research, does not deserve and certainly will not obtain an excess of first-rate material in the faculties of its institutions of higher learning.

This depressing process of initiation might prove less of a deterrent if it opened out a sure prospect of material and intellectual independence later on. But for a number of reasons, independence, the life-blood of Americans, is not commonly the lot of the university teacher. In the first place his salary at every stage is too meagre. The scholar is everywhere a man who has put the grosser prizes of acquisition behind him; but if he is to be effective in the work of his modest choice he must be paid enough to maintain his family in decent comfort without extra earnings, to be able to purchase the tools of his trade in the shape of a select library or other equipment, to have a change of scene once a year and to be able to dispense an unassuming hospitality to his students. I have not gone into the statistics, but my own observation convinces me that, except where they have a private fortune, few American university teachers are in such a position. Certainly the real earnings of the academic profession in the United States are far from what they should be. An English friend who taught for some years in America told me before I came over of a distinguished European professor settled in America who had sold his private library in order to buy an automobile. A professor dependent on a university library for the tools of his trade seemed to me so incredible a figure that I did not credit the story. I do now.

These conditions have a further effect on which I cannot, in candour, avoid saying a word. The low salaries, combined with the tendency to regard academic work as a business to be confined to "office hours," tend to cut off the professors' wives, not only from contact with the students, but from the intellectual life and interests of the university. The result is disastrous from several points of view. It renders American academic society distinctly more frivolous than that of Europe. I do not say that daylight bridge parties and country club activities are unknown in European academic circles, but they are certainly far less in evidence. Then again it encourages an atmosphere of intrigue and underhand interference on the part of those who should be the open associates of their husband's interests. And, finally, it exercises an unhealthy influence, in co-educational institutions, upon the relations between the men and women students. Into this difficult subject there is no space to enter here: suffice it to say that it is one of the aspects of American university life which is most open to criticism and most in need of sincere and plain-spoken analysis.

Nor does the American professorate enjoy assured intellectual independence. I do not wish, on this point, to range myself with the extreme watchdogs of academic freedom, nor do I believe that it is part of the ordinary duty of the university teacher to promulgate opinions, be they orthodox or heterodox, on matters of passionate ephemeral controversy. The danger to which the scholar's intellectual independence is exposed in the United States seems to me to arise not so much from the tendency to place a ban on this or that "advanced" or "radical" doctrine as from lack of understanding among those in authority as to what free intellectual activity really implies.

The teacher in an American university who is prepared to adventure with his students in the true Platonic spirit, "whithersoever the argument leads," must be ready to face the criticism and misrepresentation of the routineers, who are likely to constitute the majority of his colleagues and governors, and to endure the petty pin-pricks and obstructions of Jacks-in-office. If he has faith and courage and is prudent enough not to give battle on unessentials he can win his way through, but the process is lonely and the experience too often embittering. There are middle-aged men, and, I fancy, not a few, in American universities to-day who, had they been better supported, would by now be enjoying an international reputation and attracting transatlantic students to their classrooms. As it is, they have shrunk into themselves, cynical, disillusioned, and prematurely aged, and the students who could have found in them an inspiration see only a warning example.

Until these conditions are remedied and the emphasis placed where it belongs, on real teaching, it is clear to an outside observer that the American university, on its arts side, will too often remain a university only in name. It will, generally speaking, continue to be, for the student a finishing school, for the administration a business establishment, for the ordinary teacher a routine, for the investigator a means for supporting his researches, and for American life as a whole, in relation to the real forces of the age, a tranquil and almost stagnant backwater.

# IV

## EDUCATION AND
## INTERNATIONAL GOODWILL[1]

SOME years ago I was staying at a country house. It was a wet afternoon, my host was busy, and I was left to my own devices. Finding my way to the library, I discovered an edition of the works of Mazzini and I was deep in its study when my host returned. "Those volumes," he told me, "I owe to a friend who regards Mazzini as the inspiration of his life. As you will see by the dedication, he is eager that I should share his reverence." I turned to the flyleaf and saw the name of Earl Grey.

That is my only personal link—an indirect and fortuitous link—with that great Englishman and great internationalist.

I use the term "internationalist" advisedly, because although Earl Grey's pre-occupation was mainly with the peoples inside the British Commonwealth rather than with those whom we ordinarily regard as foreign nations, he never allowed the fact of British rule, or of his own social or official position, to obscure the necessity for sympathy, for understanding, for mutual self-respect, for the attempt to penetrate behind the uniformities of government to the diversities of national personality. That was the secret of his popularity in Canada and Australia, and that was the inspiration of the work he tried to do, not long before his

[1] Written in connexion with a Commemoration of Earl Grey at Newcastle-on-Tyne.

death, for better relations between this country and Ireland.

Mazzini was a great internationalist. Yet at the same time he was a great Italian nationalist. He believed that the road to permanent peace and real international understanding lay through the self-expression of the nations of which Humanity is composed. Humanity was for him an orchestra, in which each nation has its own appropriate instrument to play, its own distinctive contribution to make to the harmony of the whole. But at the time at which he wrote and taught, some three-quarters of a century ago, the conditions of the problem were not so clear as they have since become. I propose, therefore, to take up Mazzini's central thought, the promotion of international goodwill, to subject it to analysis in the light of experience, and to point out the spirit in which it should be approached and the methods most likely to prove successful. In other words, I propose to examine *international contacts*, and to see which of them really promote understanding and an organic relationship, and which of them, on the other hand, remain merely mechanical and sometimes even do more harm than good.

Earl Grey's county of Northumberland is the scene of what is perhaps the most successful international contact in Europe, the most successful blending of nationalism and internationalism. The relations of England and Scotland, of Englishmen and Scotsmen, based as they are on the rock of self-respect in each case, are so healthy, so normal, so organic, that we tend to forget what a problem they once presented, and how difficult it is for outsiders to understand the spirit of kindly *persiflage* which pervades them. I always remember a conversation I had with a Scottish friend about twenty years ago. He had been spending some time in Berlin. It was just after the Boer War, and he had been forced to listen to a great many unpleasant remarks in Berlin drawing-rooms about the policy of this country. But he had discovered an unfailing way of baffling these voluble critics. He would let them go on full blast and then reply, in the gentlest Lowland manner, "That is exactly what we in Scotland always say about the English!" And he would leave the Berlin Anglophobes more puzzled than ever as to how the British Empire managed to hold together.

One other preliminary remark. The problem we have to consider is that of promoting international *understanding*, not that of promoting international *love*. The problem is wrongly stated when it is placed on the emotional plane. In the early ardour of the French Revolution, the poet Schiller, addressing the peoples of the world, cried out

> Seid umschlungen, Millionen!
> Diesen Kuss der ganzen Welt.

But such a sentiment, as we all realize to-day, is nearer the ridiculous than the sublime. We shall go equally wrong if we use language which suggests that Englishmen ought to feel as tenderly and as intimately towards Americans, Frenchmen, Chinese, Arabs, and Zulus as towards their own children. We do not ask them to feel such an intimacy even towards their fellow townsmen or business colleagues. Our problem, then, is one of knitting intellectual relations, not emotional relations, of developing acquaintanceship and mutual knowledge, not the warmer feelings of friendship and affection. These may or may not follow in individual cases, or between nations which have special affinities for one another; but they are not of the essence of the problem.

How is such understanding promoted?

There is a serious danger, in this age of organisation, of our believing that we can attain the goal of international understanding by short cuts, by organized and mechanical substitutes designed to spare us the trouble of making the effort which is always needed in order to bring one human soul into touch with another. It is indeed one of the common fallacies of the age to believe that international understanding is brought about automatically, as a result of the play of impersonal forces.

Let us first look at some of these mechanical contacts and see whether, *of themselves*, they promote understanding.

The first and most obvious binding agency between peoples is government or the state. Is international understanding promoted by putting different nations under a single government? Tennyson has written of the day,

When the war-drum throbs no longer and the battle-flag is furled
In the Parliament of Man, the Federation of the World.

But is a federation, a common government, necessarily a promoter of understanding between nations? We have a striking instance to the contrary at our own doors. The union of England and Scotland has promoted understanding. The union of Great Britain and Ireland did not. Why not? Why is there, perhaps a better chance of Anglo-Irish understanding to-day under the Free State régime than there ever was under the Union? Without trespassing onto forbidden ground I think we can safely answer: it is because of the psychological factors of the problem. The Irish problem, in fact, like the problem of the relations between Sweden and Norway, was far more than a political problem. Therefore it could not be solved by the levelling effect of common political institutions.

Here I must stop to meet an objection. "The instance you have just taken," I shall be told, "is an instance of an *imposed* common government. But if peoples have agreed upon common rule, if they have voluntarily adopted a system of union or federation such a government will in time obliterate their differences." I wish I could believe this: for, if it were true, we need only fold our arms and let the Covenant of the League of Nations—which is for many purposes a common instrument of government for the members of the League—do its obliterating work. But this reasoning is too simple to be true. It overlooks the fact that peoples may agree to form a common government for all sorts of reasons, such, for instance, as fear of a third party, and that their association under such a government may be a constant process of compromise, of evading points of difficulty and disagreement, driving them down out of sight until greater dangers are out of the way. Take one very pertinent instance. The fact that the dependent peoples of the British Empire showed during the war that they preferred British rule to German rule does not in itself prove that satisfactory mutual relations have been knit between us and them. Rather should it be a spur to a new effort on our part to deepen the relationship thus revealed. An Empire held together by fear of attack is an Empire which will fall to pieces when the League of Nations can effectively relieve it from this fear, as the first British Empire in North America fell to pieces in the generation after the French had been driven out of Canada. Common government *may* remain a purely mechanical factor, or it may provide the needed opportunity for co-operation and thus for real understanding.

The same is true of the League of Nations itself. It provides an opportunity for international understanding: it does not bring it about automatically. Some of the peoples who belong to it regard it in the light of an insurance policy. But there is not much of the spirit of Mazzini in our relations with our Insurance Company. Some peoples regard it as an opportunity for limelight. We need not grudge it them; but it leaves the central problem unsolved. I have a fervent and, I hope, a reasoned faith in the League; but the most durable work that it has done hitherto is that about which least is known—the development of international co-operation and understanding, through the Secretariat, the International Labour Office, and various technical conferences, between fellow professionals in different countries.

I pass to the second of our short cuts—Trade. "Surely," I shall be told, "if you are calling for contacts between individuals rather than contacts between governments, the modern world supplies the remedy. Every year thousands and tens of thousands of relationships are knit between individual Englishmen and individual foreigners— through the agency of commerce." This was the basis of Cobden's belief in the dawn of an era of international peace. He believed that peace would be brought about through the knitting of a world-wide network of international relationships through the process of buying and selling. "The least possible intercourse between governments, the greatest possible intercourse between private individuals," was one of his favourite maxims.

Cobden has been dead a good many years and many stones have been cast at his memory by hot partisans, but his doctrine, based an the utilitarian philosophy of his day, is constantly reappearing, often in applications at which he would be greatly surprised. There are free traders of his own strict sect who call on us to break down all trade barriers in order to secure a harmonious world. There are others, like Mr. Keynes and the promoters of the Genoa Conference, who would break down all barriers in Europe, or a part of Europe, in order to secure a continent of "good Europeans." Then there are the imperialists who bid us break down all trade barriers in the British Commonwealth in order that we may have a harmonious Empire. Then there are the Americans who, having created the greatest Free State area in the world, in which the peoples of Europe can blend and melt into a single uniform nationality, expect, or rather expected until lately, that they would secure harmony without further striving. But within the last ten or fifteen years, roughly from the time of the Balkan War of 1911, the people of the United States have awoken to the fact that their nationality problems have not been solved, have indeed in some cases been intensified, by unimpeded commercial intercourse: hence the drastic new immigration policy, the latest instalment of which has just been occupying Congress. Nor, in the Great Free Trade area which we have established in India, are Indians discovering that trade serves of itself to break down political or religious differences. Nor did the Hapsburgs discover it in the Austro-Hungarian monarchy. Nor is it true of the world as a whole that commerce breeds harmony. Germany was our greatest customer before the war. Many people, Cobdenites and others, thought that this fact would always stand in the way of an Anglo-German conflict. But bills of exchange are not necessarily harbingers of goodwill, nor are commercial travellers necessarily agents of enlightenment and mutual understanding. To put the question in the concrete—have your own special commercial relations with Norway and Denmark led to special relationships of understanding with

those countries? Did Ibsen find his way to London via
Newcastle, and the Danish High Schools reach the Board
of Education by the same route? I do not know: but, if so,
it did not happen automatically, but through the work of
skilled and devoted apostles, doing for our relations with
Denmark and Norway what Sir Theodore Morison has
lately been doing for our relations with France.

I do not mean by this that trade is selfish. Trade is service; and international trade is international service. But
an international service needs constantly to bear in mind
its responsibility in respect of promoting international
understanding. This is true of diplomacy; it is true also of
commerce.

I pass to a third mechanical agency—Language. Of all
the bad short cuts towards international understanding
the idea of a common language is the most misleading—
all the more dangerous because it has a certain superficial
plausibility. Two forms of international language are
recommended to us. First there is the idea of a universal
language manufactured so as to embody the greatest common measure of a group of existing languages. On this
theory international intercourse is to be carried on by
nobody in his own language, but by everybody in an aux-
iliary language made to suit their convenience. Several
such languages have been put on the market, and some,
such as Volapük, Ido, and Esperanto, have secured numerous devotees. I have not studied any of them; so I will say
nothing against them individually. No doubt they are
marvels of the inventor's skill; and if we do not like them
we ought to remember that, as Dr. Johnson said of the
performing dog, the wonder is not that they are disap-
pointing but that the trick has been attempted at all.
Talleyrand remarked long ago that language had been

given men in order to conceal their thoughts. His dictum seems to be almost perfectly exemplified by an arrangement under which nobody is able to express his full meaning and everybody expresses a crude approximation to his meaning. A manufactured language must always be abhorrent to any student of literature or any true lover of words. It is in fact a language for manufactured people, a language for Robots.

But what of the other idea that is put forward, that of promoting world unity by the elimination of lesser languages—the languages of the less numerous or less important national groups—and concentration on a few chosen world-media of intercourse, such as English, French, Spanish, German, or Russian. There are many arguments of convenience in favour of this idea; authors would benefit by being able to appeal to a wider circle for their books; the new *lingua franca* would play the part that Latin played in the Middle Ages. Moreover, it is remarked that, by its adoption of English and French as official languages, the League of Nations has already committed itself to this policy.

This is true. The League was bound to do so for reasons of practical convenience; but it has done so at a cost. The result is that the only delegations which can be really eloquent in the Assembly are the French, the Belgians, the Irish, and the Roumanians, since no others can attain to eloquence in either of the two standard languages. No doubt we English could, but as a rule we disdain to try!

The argument for a world-language is really, at bottom, a Roman, a Prussian, or, shall we say? a Chinese argument —the argument of a mandarin who feels himself to be at the apex of a pyramid of culture extending over some three or four hundred million people and is naturally contemptuous of smaller nationalities and more provincial tongues. The case for lesser languages, for Welsh, for Norwegian, for the Bengali of Tagore, the Italian of Dante, the English of Shakespeare, rests on the fact—which the psychologists and even the biologists are coming to admit—that there is an intimate relationship between a people and its cultural inheritance, including, of course, its inherited mode of self-expression. A language is an expression of life; to destroy it is as great an act of barbarism as wantonly to destroy a living creature.

You may have been surprised that just now I spoke of English as a lesser language. But look at the natives of this island, and even at the English-speaking peoples overseas, through the Chinese mandarin's telescope and they loom small enough beside the millions of China. Moreover, go far enough back, and you will come to a time when English and its culture were as humble as the small struggling languages of to-day. In the early fourteenth century, so a contemporary Latin writer tells us, it was not considered respectable to speak English owing to the superior social prestige of Norman-French, which was like that of English in Wales a generation or two ago.[1] Then came the Hundred Years' War, together with Langland, Wiclif, and Chaucer, who saved their twentieth-century

---

[1] I am indebted on this point to an interesting address by Professor Fynes Clinton, of Bangor, reprinted in the *Welsh Outlook* for March and April, 1924. "Ranulph Higden," he says, "writing in Latin about 1350, says of English: 'This corruption of the native tongue is largely due to two causes: because the children in the schools, contrary to the custom of other nations, ever since the coming of the Normans, have abandoned their own language and are compelled to construe in French: also because the sons of noblemen in their very cradles are instructed in the French language. Hence people in the country districts, wishing to be like them, strive to the utmost to be French, that they may seem more respectable (ut per hoc spectabiliores videantur).'" In the following paragraph Professor Fynes Clinton cites a passage from M. Paul Meyer to the effect that the extinction of English, "which appeared probable at the time that Higden wrote, would have been profitable to humanity."

descendants from being brought up on a French Shakespeare, a French Milton, and a French translation of the Bible, or, in other words, made possible *an England,* an English nation, as Dante made possible an Italy, and as writers in many tongues, in Eastern Europe, in Asia, and in Africa—tongues at which we are tempted to scoff because they are poor and humble—are making possible the growth of young and vigorous nations who will some day play their full part in Mazzini's orchestra.

There is only one universal language that all men can use and understand—the language of feature and gesture. Side by side with that there are certain conventions which can be universalized, such as figures and mathematical symbols or mapmakers' signs. For the rest, there is no royal road to the understanding of nations. We can only learn to understand as many languages as possible or, better still, use the many other pathways to the understanding of nations, through their music, their art, their buildings, their customs and institutions—all the things which *reveal* the soul within, whereas a made language, and even a secondary language, only limits, distorts, and obscures.

I come to a fourth mechanical agency—travel. We English are a nation of travellers. We used to be, and still are, great explorers and adventurers; in these latter days we are great tourists also. But does travel promote international understanding? Perhaps, if we judged ourselves as tourists by the tourists of other peoples who come to us, we should say emphatically No. Consider, for instance, the kind of book which our publishers find that it pays them to produce for the tourist public—volumes in which all the stress is laid on two features, the comfortable and the picturesque, and very small consideration is given to the people, who are too often, even in countries like Italy, patronizingly described as "the natives." Take one particular instance. We were the earliest people to climb the Alps, and we have been climbing them ever since, for about 150 years. But have the hundreds of thousands of English visitors to Switzerland, and the thousands of hotels mainly peopled by the British, knit any special relationship between Britain and Switzerland? Do the names of Boecklin and Hodler, for instance, mean anything to us? Do we even know that the latter's work is represented on the Swiss banknotes with which we pay our hotel bills? What do we know of Switzerland as a democracy, or as a trilingual Commonwealth?

The fact is that travel is an art, an art of observation, of encountering new peoples and problems, of welcoming and enjoying the diversities of mankind. But the whole business of the modern tourist agency seems to be to preserve you from these thought-provoking encounters, to convey you, say, from Newcastle to Zermatt or Grindelwald with your national susceptibilities as unruffled and your comfort as undisturbed as if you were a parcel of eggs. The Englishman's shell must at all costs remain uncracked.

What is the remedy? How can we come to travel more intelligently? Would-be travellers are often advised to embark on a course of preparatory study. This brings me to my fifth and last mechanical agency—information. I am the last person in the world to decry history or any other systematic study; but to cram up facts and dates for a journey is no more enlightened or more profitable than to cram them up for an examination. The man or woman who has prepared for foreign travel in this way is no more fitted to go abroad than the man who has studied the labels in a picture gallery is to be an art critic. A little knowledge is a dangerous thing, particularly when it involves a temptation to refrain from using one's eyes, ears, and brain. Baedeker, the *Encyclopædia Britannica*, and, I would add, the *Cambridge Modern History*, are excellent servants but very bad masters. The way to the understanding of a foreign nation is not primarily through its history, or its government, or its public institutions—still less through its railway time-tables and hotel advertisements—but through its life. Sometimes its life is a living embodiment of its history—thus "Irish history," it has been said, "is for Englishmen to remember and for Irishmen to forget" —sometimes it is a reaction against it, as in present-day Italy and, to some extent, in the United States and some of our own Dominions. To know a few Italians of the younger generation is, just at this moment, a better passport to the understanding of Italy than to have Mommsen, Gibbon, and Gregorovius at one's fingers' ends. It is a great thing to be able to travel light, with little baggage, baggage of the mind as of the body. You will enjoy your library all the more when you get home.

It is time to sum up this gloomy review. Am I then opposing, you will ask, the extension of international contacts through government, commerce, travel, study, and the international language that is coming to be known as Geneva French?

By no means. I favour all these agencies. Only I say, by themselves they are not enough. Automatic internationalism is not enough. By itself it is lifeless and useless for our purpose, which is to create goodwill through understanding. It needs to be vitalized.

How can it be vitalized? I have indicated the answer in my title—by means of Education.

What is the function of education in connexion with

internationalism? Is it to teach the history of foreign nations, the geography of the five continents, modern languages, and the Covenant of the League of Nations? Yes, all this is valuable, but it is all subsidiary. The most important thing of all is for our teachers to teach their students *how to open the windows of their minds*, so that when they leave school or college they are ready to learn from life.

Many years ago a fellow student of mine who had just won a First and a Fellowship remarked to me in an unguarded moment: "Thank goodness, now I shan't have to do any more thinking!" I am sorry to have to admit that he is a Professor to-day! What he ought, of course, to have said was, "Thank goodness, now I shan't have to do any more *remembering!* I can look around and think for myself."

If our educational system is to help us in the promotion of international understanding it must become less rigid, less mechanical, less cramped by cut-and-dried requirements; above all, it must give teachers of all grades a better chance for keeping their special interests alive and refreshing them by change of scene. Our universities and our training colleges, too, if they are to justify their existence, ought to be centres of ideas, places sought after by foreigners anxious to be in contact with what is going on in our minds. Moreover, exchanges of teachers, not of university teachers only, but of secondary teachers and indeed teachers of all kinds, ought to be greatly multiplied.

What of the language difficulty? I shall be asked. We ought to look forward to the time when every teacher will know at least one foreign language well enough to be able to take a class of foreign students after a brief period in the country. Moreover, in the case of the United States and the Dominions this difficulty does not exist. Nothing is more needed to improve Anglo-American relations than a body of resident British teachers in America and of American teachers here. They would supply a standing corrective to the false impressions gathered on both sides of the Atlantic. We judge Americans by the summer visitor; and they judge us by our winter tourists, who dash through the country in sleeping-cars, from the Atlantic to the Pacific, delivering the same address, or variations on the same address, at every city on their road, and returning home with a sackful of dollars and a hearty contempt for the people of the United States. Our teachers, even at their weakest, would at least be both humbler and more conscientious than these star performers on the international stage.

There is one respect in which education has of recent years been a positive hindrance to the growth of international understanding. I refer to the development of excessive specialization at universities. When I study the prospectuses of some up-to-date institutions of learning— I am not now thinking so much of this country—I am appalled, both at the herd of professors and lecturers and at the minute subdivision of departments. Universities in some countries are coming to be organized like factories, with watertight barriers between department and department. The question has been asked as to what the Founder of Christianity would do if he came back and saw the multiplicity of sects who invoke his name. Similarly one feels inclined to ask what Plato and Aristotle would do if they came back and found the multitudinous rags and tatters into which industrious specialists have divided the seamless garment of their thought. They would have to look in a dozen or more pigeon-holes for some part of the study of their ideas; and they would find hardly any one who really understood them because hardly any one had studied them as a unity. It is said that some of the defects of that much-criticized document, the Treaty of Versailles, are due to the fact that it was drawn up by specialists, and that no single mind grasped it as a whole before its completion. It is one of the greatest dangers of modern life that we are inclined to give up the attempt to study difficult problems as a whole. We relieve our consciences by flinging parts of them to specialists who, in their turn, disclaim responsibility for general conclusions. This habit of mind is ruinous to internationalism; for to have an impression of a foreign country as a whole, of its spirit and atmosphere, is an indispensable preliminary to an understanding of its detailed problems. You can no more study France, Italy, or the United States piecemeal than you can study Plato piecemeal. I have had occasion sometimes to see the results of attempts to study Britain piecemeal, to study, for instance, our party system, or our educational system, or even intellectual and social movements like Guild-Socialism or the W.E.A., without any general knowledge of the background. I am sure that if you had read these disquisitions you would have felt as I did: "it is all so hopelessly wrong that it is impossible to know where to begin correcting it." From the technical point of view, as a thesis for a degree, such a production may be a wonderful piece of research. But it does not even "deviate into truth."

It is the old story of the operation which was completely successful, only the patient died. Do not let us murder foreign countries in this way. Let us take for our model not the specialism of the nineteenth century but rather the humanism of the sixteenth. Erasmus learned more about England through his talks with More and Colet than the thesis grubbers will ever learn in the Record Office.

But how can one get this general impression, this impalpable atmosphere of foreign countries? By a very simple means, at any rate in a sea-port and commercial centre—by improving our conditions of hospitality. If we take our professions of internationalism seriously we ought to see to the establishment, in every important city, of an international centre, at once a social club and an intellectual meeting-ground, where strangers who desired to get to know Britain and British life would be welcome. It might, perhaps, be attached to the Public Library or to the Municipal Buildings; and the entertainment, social and intellectual, ought not to be wholly to the shyer and more specialized sex. Women have not yet realized the part they can play in promoting vital international contacts. It is so much easier to go to a League of Nations Union meeting than to entertain a Dutchman or a Spaniard at tea. But the latter is real internationalism, while the former may mean a brief thrill and nothing more.

How can we secure that our international contacts shall remain real and alive? There is no fool-proof system for establishing international relations, and, when I think of a personality like Earl Grey, I am almost inclined to say "Internationalists, like poets and teachers, are born, not made." But even a born teacher may benefit by a practical suggestion, so I would venture to put forward three guiding principles.

Firstly, an international contact, to be vital, must be a contact between personalities. Each side must be itself. Do not let the Englishman try to gesticulate like a Frenchman, or encourage the Frenchman to imitate our English reserve. Our starch is real starch and is acceptable because it is real. French starch would be unreal and therefore only ridiculous. We must learn, not simply to tolerate the idiosyncrasies, what we are inclined to call the bad manners, of others, but to enjoy them. If the foreigner wants us to be ourselves, we must let him be himself, not what we think he ought to be, or what he would be if he had had an English public school education. Otherwise intercourse will merely degenerate into an exchange of the polite and meaningless formalities of which we have seen so much in the diplomacy of recent years. The old affinity between France and Scotland must have been partly based on a common regard for intellectual frankness and integrity. And is it not perhaps just that which has enabled a Socialist Premier so unexpectedly to reawaken the tradition of Mary Queen of Scots?

In the second place, a true international contact must be a contact between equals. There is no more deadly foe to international goodwill than patronage or condescension. How many a gift has been spoiled by the manner of its giving! The British and American peoples are the two most open-handed peoples in the world—but the two peoples most prone also to the defects of philanthropy. The first duty of a philanthropist, after he has given, is to know how to receive. We have a signal instance of our incapacity in this respect in our recent reluctance to let the Austrian people, in the shape of their National Opera Company, pay us back in the art in which they excel for the material aid we have rendered them. Inequality in international relations, as in social relations, always ends by injuring the superior party. An obligation unrepaid festers in the mind of the debtor. How virtuous we feel about paying our debt to the United States! We must allow other peoples the opportunity for the same rosy glow, even if they unburden themselves of their obligations in a manner which appeals to them more than it does to us.

The third principle I would lay down is what I would call *the law of greatest effort*. The real artist is never satisfied with easy achievement. The same is true of internationalism. The easy is only the stepping stone to the more difficult. I know no better illustration of my meaning than a phrase I read the other day in an article in a German newspaper by a young German graduate who recently visited Paris at the invitation of a young French League of Nations worker. The two met at the station and almost at once were deep in political discussion. "Will not collaboration between us be very difficult?" asked the German. "*Si les choses ne sont pas difficiles,*" replied the Frenchman, "*elles ne sont pas intéressantes et nous ne nous en occupons pas.*" There is the true spirit of internationalism—to make of each achievement an opportunity for scaling yet more difficult heights.

Yet how prevalent is the opposite tendency—the tendency to promote the easy contacts and ignore the rest, to concentrate on the English-speaking peoples, or the so-called Anglo-Saxon peoples, or the European peoples, or the white peoples—on any section of humanity which has something familiar to offer us as against the dark mysterious mass beyond. But no tendency could be more dangerous at the present day; for it would lead inevitably to the very perils and cleavages we are seeking to avoid. It would lead to the division of the world into *blocs* of psychologically kindred peoples, aligned according to race or civilization or material interest, whereas our whole object should be to break down these natural barriers. It is not true internationalism, for instance, but sheer laziness, to be satisfied with an Anglo-American *entente*, or rather, with a relationship between Britain and Americans of British descent. Our aim should rather be to make a living British-

American relationship an opportunity for a joint adventure into other more difficult realms.

For such a joint adventure the League of Nations affords a magnificent opportunity, and when once the United States realize what they are missing they will undoubtedly hasten to join. For the League is a living expression of the principles I have enunciated. It is a meeting-ground of real personalities, where you may witness the clash, not of interests only but of temperaments. It is a meeting of equals, great and small, rich and poor, white, brown, black, and yellow. There is no better education in international problems than to listen to its discussions and to watch the play of mind of their participants.

One last thought. It has been said that the man who makes two blades of grass grow where there was but one before is a benefactor to mankind. That was a nineteenth-century apothegm characteristic of an age which gloried in material production. We of the twentieth century have a more difficult problem before us, not the increase of the world's resources but the inter-communication of its wisdom, the interpretation of its rich diversities of national inheritance and achievement. So let us rather say "blessed is the man who has added one link to the chain of understanding wherewith we are girdling the world."

For the world of our vision is no single field of waving grain, every ear like its fellow and blown the same way by the same breeze, but an infinitely diversified landscape, seen, as an airman would see it, from above, land and sea, city and country, cornland and pasture, orchard and forest, all placed at the service of man, of a humanity united in one great community of mutual understanding.

## V

## NATIONALISM AND INTERNA-
## TIONALISM[1]

IT is a common theme among the pessimists that the
world has relapsed since the armistice into a temper
of nationalism which renders illusory the hopes and
dreams of internationalism so widely entertained during
the war. These two movements or moods, nationalism and
internationalism, are regarded as opposing and mutually
exclusive, and the very evident ascendancy of the former
is too often unquestioningly accepted as involving, if not
the final defeat, at least the indefinite postponement of
the latter. If this were really so the outlook for mankind
would be black indeed, for nationalism, not only in Europe
and America but throughout the world, is clearly a rising
power. But the belief that nationalism and internationalism are incompatibles, although superficially plausible, is
based upon ignorance of men and nations and a complete
misunderstanding of the two movements themselves. As
this belief is widespread and is acting as a serious hindrance
to the advance of a real understanding between nations, it
may be worth while to subject it to the test of a brief
analysis.

Let us look first at the complaint brought by the disillusioned idealists and anti-nationalists against the post-
war world. What is the general indictment that lurks
behind the manifold grumbling about the Balkanization of
Europe, the unreasonableness of France, the commercial-
ism of Britain, the impenitence of Germany, the self-

[1]Contributed to *Foreign Affairs*, New York, 1923.

assertion of the Little Entente states and of the British
Dominions, and the recrudescence of isolationism and
Monroeism in the United States? We are often told, when
these topics are mentioned, that the world has relapsed
from the principles and standards of internationalism into
a state of blind and unreflecting nationalism. But, when we
look at the facts, this explanation is obviously insufficient.
If nationalism were really rampant in East-Central
Europe how could the Little Entente between Czechoslovakia, Rumania, and Jugoslavia ever have come into
existence or been maintained for three years? How indeed
could these three states and their Polish neighbour, all of
them inhabited by a variety of peoples, have succeeded in
preserving their identity at all? Or how, if nationalism
were the world's ruling passion, could the British Commonwealth, with its manifold variety of peoples, have been
held together? How could France have maintained the
unity of her empire, or even of her newly integrated home
country? How could bilingual Belgium and trilingual
Switzerland have survived? How, finally, could the United
States have avoided serious conflicts with the unassimi-
lated nationalisms of millions of her recent arrivals?
Clearly, even if we grant that nationalism has been one of
the forces at work, it has not been the most powerful and
determining factor. What we really find, when we examine
the counts of the indictment against the post-war world
more closely, is that the policies complained of are quite as
marked in the case of states consisting of several nations
acting in co-operation as in those consisting of but a single
nation. The real trouble in fact is not nationalism, in any
of the many forms which that movement is capable of
assuming, but something which may be described by the
less romantic and more comprehensive designation of

selfishness. In other words, the indictment should be drawn not against nations but against states; not against statesmen acting as the spokesmen of nationalities and the interpreters of nationalism but against statesmen acting as the instruments of sovereign states, great or small, uni-national or multi-national; not against Mr. Lloyd George as a Welshman, M. Briand as a Breton, President Masaryk as a Slovak, M. Venizelos as a Cretan, but against the policies of the British Empire, the French and Czecho-slovak Republics and the Kingdom of Greece.

Some such relapse into selfish policies was almost in-evitable after the strain of war and of war-time co-opera-tion. We are not concerned here with its details or degrees —with the question whether it would have been possible, by wiser and more far-sighted statesmanship, to have pre-vented the pendulum from swinging back so far. What is important for our present purpose is to note that the existing political troubles of the world arise, not from the passions of nations but from the policies of states, and that it is with the adjustment of these policies, not with the sublimation of national passions, that constructive political work in the field of foreign affairs is concerned. Internationalism, in the political sense in which the word is customarily used, is in fact concerned with promoting the co-operation of states, not with controlling or even canalizing the undue self-expression of nations. It is un-fortunate that this vital truth should be concealed by the vagaries of our political terminology. The League of Nations is, of course, a misnomer. It is a League of States, and it will be subject to perpetual misunderstanding if it is thought of as anything else. If its membership is extended to Ireland and not to Scotland, to Haiti and not to the Afro-American nation, it is because Ireland and Haiti have a distinct political status which Scotland and the negroes of the American continent cannot claim.

The work of internationalism, then—or, as it would be more properly called, the work of inter-state organization —is concerned with the mutual relations of sovereign bodies, however composed, and has nothing directly to do with the relations of nations.

From this it would appear that internationalism and nationalism, so far from being conflicting forces, do not impinge upon one another at all, and that the current impression to the contrary is completely unfounded. Nevertheless there is no smoke without fire and it will probably be felt that the above summary analysis does less than justice to the common view. Theoretically and in principle, it will be said, the two movements dwell on separate planes and ought not to conflict. But in point of fact they frequently do. Both in Europe and America there is a large admixture of what cannot be described otherwise than as nationalist sentiment in the conduct of affairs of state. To explain why this is so and to understand its significance we must subject the whole movement of nationalism to closer scrutiny.

It is difficult for a European to discuss this subject with Americans, not merely because of the differences in current nomenclature which have already been mentioned, but because the whole course and direction of national sentiment has been different on the two sides of the Atlantic. The nations of the American continent, north and south, are not only far younger than the nations of Europe, but they have also come into existence through a wholly different historical process. Nevertheless the resultant sentiment of nationalism is of much the same character in America as in Europe, and the likeness will undoubtedly become more marked as the accidents of origin are smoothed out by the normal processes of development and the life of the two continents tends more and more to beat with a similar pulse and rhythm. The nationalism of America, or at any rate of the United States of America, to use a phrase of Mr. Van Wyck Brooks, is coming of age. The difference between fifteen and twenty-five in the life of an individual is akin to the difference between one century and three or four in the life of a nation. When the youth of fifteen has come to forty and the man of twenty-five has touched fifty, the common element in their experience becomes much more apparent. The same will be true of the inner experience of the nations of Europe and America as the generations go on.

What is nationalism? It is a movement or manifestation of the sentiment of nationality. It is often employed in a derogatory sense to denote a violent, intolerant and even aggressive manifestation; but it may equally well be employed of manifestations of a more equable temper. It will, however, conduce to clearness in the discussion to set aside the term nationalism and to deal rather with "nationality" and "nation" than with their manifestations in "nationalist" movements of various types. "Nationality," then, is the group-consciousness of which nationalism is one of the outward expressions; and a nation is a body of people bound together by the particular form of group-consciousness described as "nationality" or "the sense of nationality."

What is this particular form of group-consciousness which constitutes nationality? What is it that distinguishes a nation or body of people held together by a sentiment of nationality from other human groups and corporate bodies? It is easier to say what a nation is not than to define satisfactorily what it is. As we have seen, it is not a state or political body. The English nation is something different from the British Commonwealth and (though this is not so commonly recognized) the American nation is something different from the American Commonwealth. English nationality does not necessarily imply British citizenship, nor did Henry James cease to be an American when he surrendered his American citizenship during the war. Again, a nation is not a church or religious body. Turkish nationality is something different from Mohammedanism and Jewish nationality is something different from Judaism. It is true that practically all Turks are Moslems and that many, if not most, of those who share the sentiment of Jewish group-consciousness share also in the Jewish religious belief and observances; but the distinction between church and nation, though frequently denied by Jews, as the distinction between commonwealth and nation is denied by Americans, is nevertheless undeniable.

Again, a nation is not a territorial unit. There are probably more Irishmen outside Ireland, more Norwegians outside Norway, more Jews outside Palestine, perhaps also more Scotsmen, Slovaks, and Letts outside Scotland, Slovakia, and Latvia than in the compact area of territory with which their national sentiments are related.

Again, a nation is not a race. None of the existing nations, not even those who, like the Jews, have laid most stress on purity of stock, correspond to the racial divisions and subdivisions of the anthropologists. The attempts made at repeated intervals by anti-Semitic writers such as Houston Stewart Chamberlain in Germany and less doctrinaire and more frankly abusive writers in America, to enlist racial prejudice in the cause of nationalist intolerance spring from pure obscurantism.

Finally, a nation is not a linguistic unit. The English-speaking peoples, whether under the Union Jack or not, are, with one exception, not English; neither are the German-speaking Swiss and Austrians German, nor the French-speaking Swiss and Belgians and Canadians French. Conversely, cases occur in which national sentiment exists not only, as in English-speaking North America and Australasia, without a national medium of expression, but without any common medium of expression at all. Among Welshmen, for instance, there is a large mass who know no Welsh and a very considerable body who know no English, and the same phenomenon can be found on a smaller scale in Ireland. Thus these two bodies of Welshmen and Irishmen, each of them participating consciously and deliberately in the deep-lying sentiment of their nationality, have no means of communicating with one another in speech—an example which is striking not so much for the light it throws on the vicissitudes of Welsh and Irish history as for the revelation it affords of the inadequacy of words as a means for the expression of thought. Another example of the same kind is the survival of the Jewish national consciousness in spite of the varieties of Jewish speech. A heroic effort is now indeed being made to revivify Hebrew and make it the current speech of the Jewish homeland in Palestine. This experiment, like the parallel experiment in Ireland, may possibly succeed, but it is possible that such success may be accompanied by a narrowing and stiffening of the national soul. On the other hand it may fail; but its failure, whilst in some ways regrettable, would certainly not entail the disintegration of the Jewish national personality, which has survived far deeper disappointments during its long and chequered career. The fact is that we are only at the beginning of the

study of the inter-relations between language and personality, whether individual or national. Students of
phonetics, of music, and of psychology have yet to join
hands in investigating the sub-conscious region whence
proceed the infinite variations of pitch and intonation, of
idiom, metaphor and symbolism, of gesture and phonation
which, to the student of modes of human expression, are
like a warm covering of flesh and blood over the bare
skeleton of a mere vocabulary.

If a nation is neither a state nor a church nor a race nor
a geographical or linguistic unit, what is it? No definition
is satisfactory in a matter which goes so deep or has such
wide-spread ramifications, but the following put forward
by the present writer some years ago, may at least serve as
a working basis: *a nation is a body of people united by a
corporate sentiment of peculiar intensity, intimacy and
dignity, related to a definite home country.*

National sentiment is intense: men feel towards their
nation as towards something which plays a large part in
their life and inner experience. How intense this feeling is
can be tested by the joy which every normally constituted
man feels when, after sojourning in a strange atmosphere,
he is once more brought into contact with his nationality,
whether it be in a gathering in a strange country or on his
return to his territorial base. The Englishman who feels a
catch in his throat when he sees the white cliffs of Dover
after an absence in distant lands (whether under the Union
Jack or not) and the American who raises his hat to salute
the Statue of Liberty as he steams into New York har-
bour, are both giving expression, not to their sense of
patriotism or state obligation, but to their sense of
nationality.

National sentiment is intimate: whether it be mainly

compounded of influences of heredity (as in Europe) or of environment, as in the older Americans, or whether it be something newly acquired and deliberately cherished as among the new arrivals, it is something that goes deep down into the very recesses of the being. Europeans are accustomed to believe that nationality is something so intimate that it cannot be acquired; nationality to them is akin to the family; it is the element of heredity which is paramount. Americans on the other hand are accustomed to the idea of an acquired nationality, but perhaps do not always sufficiently realize how intimate such an acquirement may be. The nationality of a European and the nationality of a recent American may perhaps be compared to a man's relation to his parents and his relation to his wife. Both sentiments are intimate; both can legitimately be compared, in the sphere of personal relations, to the sense of nationality in the wider sphere of corporate relations. But the one is hereditary, the other is elective. The European and the older American are born into their nation; the recent American has chosen his nationality and attached himself to it as to a wife. And, as parentage and marriage both go to make up a complete personality, so nationality, even among members of the older nations, will not be complete without an element of election and deliberation, or, to use a more appropriate term which the war brought home to so many, re-dedication.

National sentiment is dignified: it is on a larger and grander scale than a man's feeling towards a country or a parish, a club or a group of professional or other intimates, however warm such a feeling may be. No outsider can judge at what point a group attachment related to a definite territory reaches the degree of dignity entitling it to be described as national. Is Malta the home of a nation or is it a mere municipal port of call? Is Newfoundland the home of a nation or a mere elderly colony? Was Virginia ever a nation? Was the Old South ever a nation? Every student of these problems of sentiment must make these nice valuations for himself. In general we can only say that a nation is a nation, however small its territory, when its members feel it to be one and bear themselves accordingly. "It is not walls but men that make a city," said the Greek orator long ago; and it is not space and population but a sense of great things experienced in the past and greater lying before in the future, if we may thus deepen the implication of a phrase of Renan's, which constitutes the soul and consciousness of a nation.

Every nation has a home. The sentiment of nationality cannot gather simply round an idea or a memory or a programme or about some function or status, such as a priesthood or an aristocracy or a Legion of Janissaries. That does not mean that membership in a nation, participation in its common life and consciousness, necessarily involves residence within a fixed area, or contact with it by visits or economic ties. Consciousness can overleap the barriers and ignore the qualifications fixed by political authority for the world of statehood. No period of residence for naturalization is required to relate an Emmet born in New York to Ireland, or Theodor Herzl the Viennese journalist to Palestine, or to defer the acceptance by America of the whole-hearted offering of mind and spirit made by so many of those lately landed on her shores. But without the element of environment, the actual physical territory and what man has made of it, to form the framework and receptacle, as it were, of the national ideal, the sentiment of nationality would lose the warmth and concreteness which constitute so large a part of its appeal and

would disappear into the clouds which have swallowed up
so many unattached idealisms in the past.

We have defined nationality. Let us now observe it in
operation in various parts of the world.

It is often said that the nineteenth century witnessed
the dawn of nationality in Europe. Of some parts of
Europe this may be true, but of Western and Central
Europe, to which this judgment is usually applied, it is
certainly untrue. Englishmen were already Englishmen in
the days of Chaucer and Langland, and the France of
Froissart and Villon was already France. So, too, Dante's
Italy, though still only lisping Italian, was Italy and, in
spite of the unhappy vicissitudes and backwardness of
German political history, the men for whom Luther translated the Bible were already Germans. The history of the
rise of the different European nationalities, from Ireland
in the west to the various Slav and Baltic peoples in the
east, would form a fascinating study, intertwined as it is
with the influence of orthodoxy and heresy—where would
Bohemia be without its Hussites or Slovakia without its
Lutherans?—of music and folk-song, of backward-looking
romanticism and forward-looking idealism, of intellectual
leadership, from the universities and elsewhere, in history
and philology (as in Fichte's amazing panegyric on the
German language), in literature, geography, and archae-
ology. But until the French Revolution, this history is,
broadly speaking, non-political. Government being still
almost everywhere regarded, according to the feudal
tradition, as the concern of a special class, the people, in
whom the national consciousness was alive or in process
of formation, did not concern itself with what are now-a-
days loosely described as "national" problems and policies. The territorial lords of Europe, kings and electors

and grand-dukes and bishops and petty barons, fought and plotted and intrigued, extended their frontiers hither and thither by conquest, marriage and barter and turned the balance of power this way and that without enlisting in their causes (which would hardly bear too close a scrutiny), the deep-lying passions and sentiments which were growing up in the hearts of the populations from whom they drew tribute. It was in England and Holland that nationality was first enlisted in the political field, but it was the great outburst of the French Revolution which mingled and muddied the two streams and brought about a confusion of thought and a perplexity in action from which the world, on both sides of the Atlantic and of the Pacific, has not yet recovered.

When President Wilson, picking up a phrase from the great mischief-maker Lenin, flung the slogan of "self-determination" into the world's arena he was using a word capable of many interpretations. But the majority of mankind, under the influence of vague nineteenth-century shibboleths, understood him to be associating himself with the doctrine that every nation has a right to be a sovereign state. "It is in general a necessary condition of free institutions," said John Stuart Mill, "that the boundaries of governments should coincide in the main with those of nationalities." What Mill thus cautiously stated as a maxim of convenience (how in all sincerity could an inhabitant of the United Kingdom of England, Scotland, Wales, and Ireland put it any higher?) had long since been elevated by more ardent liberals into a gospel of indefeasible right. The necessary result of such a doctrine, as Lenin foresaw and desired, was disintegration— the break-up of that bourgeois nationalist society which he so detested.

A survey of the workings of political nationalism and of the theory of self-determination is instructive. A gospel that claims to be of universal validity and application can only show results in a limited region of Europe and Western Asia. It has helped to break up the Austro-Hungarian Empire, but it has left tri-national Switzerland untouched; it has disintegrated Russia—if indeed, for most Russians, there ever was, in the deepest sense, a Russia—but it has not brought independence either to Armenia or the Ukraine. It has torn Southern Ireland from Westminster, but has left Scotland, Wales, and Ulster where they were. It has taken German-speaking Alsace from the German Empire and restored it to France; it has rescued the Germanic peasants of Flanders from their invading kinsmen and reunited them with their French-speaking fellow-citizens. It has destroyed the dream of an Illyrian Republic and brought a joint Serbo-Croatian-Slovenian Kingdom into existence. Finally, having demolished three autocratic empires, it has left the indescribably heterogeneous and multi-national dominion of Britain standing upright amid the débris of imperialisms. In other words, national sentiment, whilst proving an invaluable ally for a movement of resistance against the abuses of misgovernment, as in Austria-Hungary, or against the pin-pricks of misunderstanding, as in Ireland, is unable by its own unaided efforts to make the political map conform more nearly to its pattern design.

Turn now to America. What application can be found, either in North or South America, for Mill's doctrine? Here it is not a question of redrawing a political map so as to carve new frontiers to fit old and existing nations. It is a case of fitting nations into existing frontiers, or rather of helping nations to find themselves and be themselves within the fixed framework of an established political society. The malady of Europe has not arisen, as is so often said, from its nationalisms. It has arisen from a simpler cause, from bad government. Europeans have had to wage a long fight, of which the recent war, we may hope and believe, is the last phase, against autocracy and its consequent injustice, not against the denial of "rights" to "nations," but against the denial of justice and liberty to men and women. The malady of America, on the other hand, the growing restlessness and perplexity of which every student of the United States must be conscious, arises not from bad government (Europe has had to suffer more, in these last years, than America from the defects of the American constitutional machine), but from its nationality problem or problems. It sounds paradoxical, yet it is substantially true to say that each continent has wrongly diagnosed its malady. The Europeans who have given their lives, from Ireland to Poland and the Ukraine, for the cause of self-determination and an independent national republic have been waging a hopeless battle for an unrealizable ideal. In all three countries, diverse as is their present status, Mill's coincidence of government with nationality is a practical impossibility. What their champions have really been fighting for, if they only knew it, has been conditions of government which would enable them to be themselves—in other words, for the supreme political goods, for Justice and Liberty,—Justice and Liberty for all dwellers in Ireland, for all dwellers in Poland and the Ukraine, irrespective of race, religion or nationality.

Americans, on the other hand, who have been much concerned in recent years over the external problems of their community life, are beginning to look back on their muck-raking campaigns with an uneasy sense that they

have not probed the real roots of the national dissatisfaction. It is true that American government and American
society leave much to be desired; but surely the real
problems of America are national, belong, that is, to the
intimate region of mind and spirit which has been spoken
of above. Let Europe, from Galway to Lemberg, from
Algeciras to Helsingfors, consolidate its newly established
democracies, establish firm guarantees of mutual protec-
tion among its states, reduce its infantile mortality, intro-
duce labour-saving science into its homes and factories and
ameliorate its plumbing. These are the tasks, practical and
positive, whether high or humble, for a continent, such as
Europe now is, of self-conscious and satisfied nationalism.
America's domestic problems are of a different order. They
are not so much political and social (the tasks in this
region are clearly indicated and not difficult of accomplish-
ment by an energetic and organizing people,) as national
in the deepest sense—to work inwards from the influences
of environment to the unalterable values of heredity, to
discover the quality and substance of the diverse populations that have married themselves to this great continent, and to make the men and women and, still more
the children, who have entered into the new national consciousness feel at home and at ease, in the deepest region
of their manifold natures, in the home of their choice.

Once the problems of nationality and the problems of
statehood and citizenship have been disentangled, they
will easily yield to treatment. It is from their century-
old confusion that so much mischief and bloodshed have
arisen, whether in the insane German design to base the
dominion of the world on the "culture," that is, the
intimate expression of a single people, or in the futile and
suicidal efforts, now happily discredited, of the straitest

sect of "Americanizers." The way is becoming clear, then, both in Europe and America, for a real internationalism, in the truest and purest sense of the word.

For internationalism, properly understood, is not contact between states; nor is it contact between supernationalists and cosmopolitans who have torn themselves loose from affiliation with their nation. It is at home neither round the green table of the diplomatists nor "above the mêlée" with the minority minds. True internationalism is contact between nations in their highest and best and most distinctive representatives and manifestations. The true contact between the West European national triangle which is so disquieting the world must be a contact, not between trust-magnates or labour-leaders or even statesmen from the three countries, but, so to speak, between Shakespeare, Molière and Goethe. It is the most characteristic figures of a national literature who are also the most international, and it is through them that understanding must come. Our efforts at internationalism have failed hitherto because they have followed the line of least effort. Any fool can book a ticket for a foreign country, just as any fool can learn Esperanto. But contacts so established effect nothing. They tell us no more than that the German or the Frenchman is a human being, a father, a workman and a lover of beer or coffee, which we knew before. It is through a deeper exploration and enjoyment of the infinite treasures of the world's nationalities, by men and women whose vision has been trained and sensibilities refined because they themselves are intimately bound up with a nation of their own, that an enduring network of internationalism will some day be knit and a harmony of understanding established in a world of unassailable diversity.

# VI

## THE SCHOLAR IN PUBLIC AFFAIRS[1]

EORGE LOUIS BEER was the *beau idéal* of a scholar
in public affairs. He made his influence felt at the
moment and in the manner in which it was most
needed; and his loss has left a gap, not only in American
but in international affairs, which it is impossible to fill.
His was a pivotal influence. Though the world little knew
it, he was one of the Indispensables—a title too often
bestowed upon noisy figures of the foreground to whom it
least belongs. Much has happened since his departure
which would assuredly have gone otherwise had he stayed.
But of this and indeed of the range and scope of his work
and its effects the present writer is not qualified to speak.
He will best fulfil the mission entrusted to him if he attempts to embody his own personal sense of admiration
and bereavement in an estimate of the function and service
of which George Louis Beer, as he saw him, for the first
and last time in Paris in June, 1919, lives in his memory
as a permanent and inspiring exemplar.

What is the place of the scholar in public affairs? There
is a venerable tradition, not yet extinct in our seats of
learning, and tracing back its origins to Plato and Aristotle,
that there is no place at all. The lover of wisdom, said
Plato, in an oft-quoted passage written no doubt at a
moment of confusion and disillusionment not unlike that
through which we are passing today, had best be hidden

---

[1]Contributed in 1921 to *George Louis Beer, a Tribute to His Life and Work in the Making of History and the Moulding of Public Opinion.* (The Macmillan Company, New York, 1924.)

under the hedge until reason reappears upon the public scene. The world has no ears for his message; he had better keep it for the elect. And Aristotle, too, on one side of his doctrine, through his sharp distinction between the "practical" and "theoretical" planes of life, and their respective careers, lent encouragement to the same inclinations of seclusion and monasticism. Prophets and preachers of city-state patriotism as they were, Plato and Aristotle became, nevertheless, partly through this strain in their doctrine, partly through the course of events which swept away their political constructions, the originators of a school of thought or a tradition which divorced the scholar from the state and immured him, first in a monastery and then in a University.

That there was sound reason for this traditional view of the scholar's part no one will deny who reflects how tender is the plant of Truth, and how likely to perish amid the buffetings of circumstance in a world where power and riches, force visible and invisible, hold sway. The humanities and the sciences, the disinterested curiosity and devotion of the seeker after truth for its own sake, survived through centuries of intellectual chaos and superstition because, here and there in the community, there were homes of quiet where students, unconscious of the tramping of armed men at their doors, lived the life of the mind and the spirit. In the long roll of years, between the five and twelve hundreds, roughly between Boethius and Abelard, to be a scholar was to be a "religious"; and, in the centuries that followed, the Universities carried on the same tradition of the scholar's place in society. With rare exceptions, of whom Erasmus is the most conspicuous, the Renaissance and post-Renaissance scholar remained secluded in his ivory tower, pursuing studies unintelligible to the multitude and desiring, not so much to influence the outside world by his ideas and discoveries as to be left in peace to worship the goddess of truth, or to enjoy the privileges of his learned corporation, as he and his fellows thought fit.

With the effect of this mode of living and thinking upon the study of the natural sciences we are not concerned. Modern life offers so many tempting prizes to those who are willing to apply scientific discovery to lucrative ends that it may perhaps plausibly be argued that the world in which Newton and Copernicus lived and thought was more favourable to the ideal of the man of science than the society in which Einstein and Marconi are featured in daily journals. But of the humanities it can be stated emphatically that, confined to the ivory tower, they are no longer humanities. Literature, philosophy, history, economics, and, above all, politics cannot be studied sincerely and truthfully from behind Common Room curtains or in a secure and padded little world whither the heartbeat of reality can rarely penetrate. All experience goes to prove that the detachment thus secured is not detachment at all but a disguised and unconscious partiality. In the study of man, man tragical or comical, man economical, man political, no accumulation of documents can act as proxy for man himself, and there is a difference of life and death, of reality and dry-as-dust, between the thoughts and writings of those who have adventured with eager inquiring mind into the heated arena of affairs and those who have sat by, connoisseur-like, notebook in hand, to mark and "interpret" the issue without living experience of the conflict.

George Louis Beer was no philosopher of the ivory tower. He was "a man of the world": he lived in the world, and his thoughts were derived from close observation of the world. But, while he was thus free from the taint of monasticism, he was equally fortunate in his avoidance of its more fashionable opposite—the temptation to subordinate truth to propaganda.

For the mediæval scholar freedom from the partialities and prejudices of the ephemeral world around him was secured by his seclusion in monastery or university. It is one of the ironies of the whirligig of time that, increasingly both in Europe and North America, such freedom is now best ensured not by being attached to seats of learning but by remaining independent of their connections and obligations. The University of today is no longer an autonomous learned corporation pursuing its life independently of the community in which it happens to be placed. It is part and parcel of a system of "national" education, and, as a general rule, as part of the scheme of the national life, its hall-mark is desired, or even required, for entrance to the teaching professions. Its government, too, in many cases, is influenced and even controlled, by the public authority. There are thus frequent and subtle occasions of interaction between the world of government and the world of learning, and the scholar, emancipated from the ivory tower, is exposed to temptations of another kind to which he has too often in recent times succumbed. In the Germany of the ex-Kaiser, for instance, it was difficult, and in Prussia practically impossible, for a professor of politics, economics, or modern history to give expression to other than orthodox views both as regards the foreground and the background of current events. To be "gesinnungstüchtig" was a *sine qua non* not only for promotion but for unmolested occupation of a post already attained; and the parrot-chorus of professors accompanying every move of German policy before and during the war will be remembered as a glaring example of the danger of descending from the ivory tower to the arena. Many of the ninety-three signatories of the famous manifesto of the German intellectuals at the outbreak of the war have since retracted with the admission that they were imperfectly informed as to the matters at issue; but what a prostitution of place and name is involved in this reckless obedience to governmental command or suggestion! Nor is this sapping of intellectual integrity confined to autocracies. Democracy, with its jealous and increasing control over seats of learning aided by public funds, is quite equally capable of playing the inquisitor or the dictator, and not only in the United States, where liberal public opinion has become alive to the danger, but in Britain also, independence of thought and freedom of expression are liable to be hampered by considerations of expediency from which old-fashioned scholars were free.

From all this medley of influences, of action and reaction, of temptations to orthodoxy and impulses of protest and rebellion, George Louis Beer was mercifully free. He was what the Germans call a "Privatgelehrter," a scholar independent in every sense materially as well as spiritually; and thus, when the moment came, he was all the freer to serve his country, and his learning and counsel were all the more valued because all the world knew that they were the sterling contributions of a free spirit.

Let us now look a little more closely at the characteristics of the type of scholar of whom George Louis Beer will be remembered as a distinguished representative.

The scholar in public affairs is not a statesman. He remains, through all activities and vicissitudes, a scholar. His main object, that is, is not to carry on public affairs but to understand them and interpret them to others.

When Thucydides commanded at Amphipolis he was the Thucydides, the same observant, reflective, and disinterested mind, that later wrote the history, including the record of his own misadventure; and when Beer sat in the Hotel Crillon at Paris, a father in counsel to the younger men and a very present help in moments of perplexity to the older, he was assuredly thinking, not only of the colonial and other problems on which his advice was sought, but on all the deeper meaning of the scene around him, of the New World at grips with the legacy of the Old World's problems, of the contact of minds and of civilizations, and of the vista of problems, and the tasks of understanding and interpretation, thus opened up. The difference between the scholar and the statesman in public affairs is that the latter is concerned, necessarily concerned as a rule, with the foreground, whilst the former spends his busy official day in ever present realization of the background. Just as Thucydides, alone among the Greeks of his generation, came to his war-work with a scientific understanding of the early history of his country at his command, so that, perhaps for the first time in the history of the human mind, he could place the events through which he was living in their setting of time and space, so Beer came to Paris with a historical and philosophical equipment which gave added emphasis to every affirmation and added force to every judgment. Yet, in a sense, the affirmation and the judgment, the advice as to this or that course of policy and action, were, in the scholar's mind, but of secondary importance; for he knew, better than the politicians and journalists who were so ready to work out or write up his opinions, how little the actions of statesmen could deflect the slow steady march of impersonal, or rather multi-personal, forces and how far more important it was, especially in the complex swift-moving world of today, to understand the powers of the age, than to seek to dominate and subject them. The world has moved strangely far from the hopes and schemes of the United States Delegation of 1919; but Beer, of all men, would be the least disappointed and disillusioned. He would see, in the unexpected sequel to the work on which he and his colleagues spent their strength, not the arbitrary hand of accident, or of domestic faction or foreign folly or wickedness, but the complex interaction and working out of forces which it is our business neither to deplore nor to despise, but to understand. Thus the scholar is always stronger than the statesman, for he is always forearmed against failure. The disaster which, by postponing his hopes and negating his too hasty ideals, is apt to turn the statesman into a cynic or a demagogue is to the scholar but a fresh and even inspiring stimulus to a new and deeper task of understanding. Have forces for which he made no allowance surged up and spoiled his reckoning? There are new vistas open for exploration, new material for the great volume, ever being composed in the mind if not on paper, on contemporary history, the true nature and deeper forces of the world in which his brief span of human life is set.

Beer's background, like that of Thucydides, was predominantly historical, and it is in this that the scholar in public affairs is distinguished from that other type, with whom he is constantly in conflict or rivalry, the philosopher. The scholar in public affairs is a Realist; he has his feet on the rock of fact, of world facts. He has learned to orientate himself, not according to some inner light related perhaps to the stars, but unrelated to the world in which we live our daily lives, but according to the march and movement of forces operating broadly in the world around him. For him, at any rate as the starting point in his journey of exploration, the familiar landmarks hold: Europe and America, capitalism and socialism, nationalism and internationalism, are part of his mental furniture. He speaks the same language as the statesmen and the democratic public, though his words and thoughts may cut deeper. He builds on the same foundations, though his yard and rule may be ampler than theirs. And thus, unlike the philosopher, who sets up his utopia in an uncharted wilderness that will never be marked on the plain man's map, he can carry men with him in his thinking. He may go fast and far, but at least the first stage of his journey is along a familiar road.

Yet the scholar, if he is to be true to his inspiration, must give rein to his curiosity, whether men can follow him or not. Thucydides, the first and greatest scholar in public affairs, and the master of realists, began indeed as a historian: but he ended as a psychologist. He began with his contemporaries, but he far outran them. And the same, in a lesser degree, will always hold good of all true scholars who adventure into public affairs resolved to continue learning and thinking and not to prostitute their equipment to purely ephemeral ends. The mistake of the idealists is to suppose that the study of human nature *in vacuo*, apart from time and circumstance, is the right starting point for the understanding of human life. Human history is indeed unintelligible without a study of human nature; but the study of human nature is the last, not the first, stage of the journey. Whatever may be true of the poet, or of other artists who work rather by intuition than by reflection, the scholar, in the true sense of the word, must of necessity proceed from the outer inwards, from the seen and human to the unseen and unknown, from the life of man in society to the life of the soul and spirit, in a word, from history to philosophy. It is only after a long and laborious exploration that he can feel as much at home in the private and secluded underworld of subconsciousness, whence so many chains of causation are set in movement, as in the imposing outward world of public affairs, which formed the starting point of his study.

There is another mark of statesmanship which belongs to the scholar in public affairs. He has the sense and touch of a living issue—that unmistakable power which the French, more sensitive than ourselves, entitle *flair*. Just as it falls to the statesman, laying down the programme of his party for a campaign or an election, to select this or that subject on which to concentrate the popular mind, so the scholar is quickened in his choice of study and contemplation by the importance which this or that topic is likely to assume in the public life of his country or of the world. Philosophers may select their subjects for their intrinsic interest to a solitary mind; thus Scotus Erigena, that classic example of detachment, was no doubt true to his inner light when he spent himself on a book which only became topical enough to excite controversy and condemnation four centuries after his death. The historian's mind moves in a different orbit. Beer's choice of the Old Colonial System as a subject for research must have borne an inner relation from the first to present-day problems of imperialism and commercial policy, and his association with the studies of *The Round Table*, and in particular with the work of Mr. Lionel Curtis, bore witness to his sense that, sooner rather than later, the constitutional problem of the British Empire must emerge into the foreground of public discussion. On both these issues his vision was prophetic, so that when the moment came he was forearmed with facts and reasonings and was able to make his book on *The English-Speaking Peoples* far more than a useful *livre d'occasion*. It will be a matter of perpetual regret that we have not been fated to watch the movement of his mind in these crucial post-war years, when problems deeper than constitutional and more testing for courage and insight even than commercial are calling to students on both sides of the Atlantic for study and formulation.

There is, however, an essential difference, on which it is worth while dwelling for a moment, between the *flair* of the scholar and of the statesman. The statesman, or at least the politician, exercises his sixth sense, his gift of political divination, by a kind of blind unanalyzed intuition. Knowing his countrymen from long experience, he is able, almost without conscious effort, to project his mind into theirs and to anticipate their reactions; all that he need do is to think away the particular knowledge and official experience which have been available to him and not to them. This kind of *flair* is found, in greater or lesser degree, in almost all persons who have occupied, for any considerable period, a public position. Queen Victoria, for instance, possessed it, although she never had to face an election. In itself, it is a useful, indeed almost an indispensable part of the statesman's equipment; but if it is not supplemented by a knowledge, at least equally well-grounded, of the real basis of affairs, as opposed to the popular idea as to their basis, it may become a danger, and even a national incubus. To know what people are saying may be the sole business of a newspaper magnate intent on selling his copy—though even this may be doubted—but it is certainly not enough for a statesman.

Very different is the *flair* of the scholar. To begin with, he is concerned, always and everywhere, not only with *what* people think but with *why* they think as they do. He explores the whole background of their state of mind. And then again, what is even more important, his *flair*, based as it is upon knowledge and not upon unanalyzed experience, is not sharply bounded by the frontiers of his own country or even province. Holding the whole world consciously in his field of vision, he can balance Europe against America, Islam against Christendom, the working class against the captains of industry, the speechless multitude against the vociferous criers in the marketplace. This is the real *flair*—not to follow, or anticipate, the cry of the moment, but to be able, from a quiet desk in New York, or a busy office in Paris, to look into the hearts and minds of millions of plain human beings in five continents and to measure the effects of this or that project of statesmanship upon their humble but multitudinous purposes.

We pass to another element in the scholar's equipment —his integrity. It is one of the chief tasks of the scholar in public affairs to maintain, and to encourage others to maintain, as high a standard of truthfulness, truthfulness of thought as well as of fact, on the platform as in the study, in the official memorandum as in the academic essay. This is indeed the first indispensable step in the long and difficult process of applying to public affairs the standards and obligations of private life. Where there is no regard for truth, where phrases and figures are twisted to serve momentary ends, where the expert is used not as a public servant but as a partisan advocate, where, in fact, wilful ignorance and falsehood have entered in and made their home in public places, there is no room for the scholar. For the scholar exists to give freely of his best to the public cause; and where he has no assurance that his services will be utilized in the spirit in which he offers them, where the gifts of his mind are liable to be prostituted for other than public ends, he had best withdraw his aid. Happily Beer was never placed before so painful a decision. But those who worked with him know how high was his standard of intellectual honesty and accuracy and how unflinchingly he maintained it. And they are in a position to measure the value, in an official society, of the leavening power of a scholar's truthfulness. The politician, in cheating others, may even in time come to cheat himself. The scholar, having learned through severe self-discipline not to allow his own mind and soul to be cheated, has neither the power nor the desire to practise deception upon his fellowmen.

One last characteristic must be touched upon, for Beer would surely not have it omitted. The scholar in public affairs, however detached and philosophic in outlook, is before all things a patriot. If he is willing and cares to serve his country, it is because he loves her and believes in her. Beer was a good American. And it was just because he was a good American that he did not shrink from investigating the origins of the Republic and revising, where truth required it, an unduly one-sided version of early American history, just as Masaryk, equally scholar and equally patriot, earned the almost unanimous displeasure of the land he later liberated by demolishing the credibility of some of its most cherished records. Where truth and patriotism are in conflict, truth must necessarily have precedence. But in fact, they are never in conflict; for, seen in the right perspective, a country's love of truth is part and parcel of its inheritance and its greatness, and a community which thinks itself compelled to sacrifice truth for any national interest is halfway on the road to decadence. Beer's Americanism was made of sterner stuff than the apologies of some of our up-to-date propagandists. The America that he worked for was an America proud and upright, honourable and self-reliant, demanding from others no more than she imposed on herself; and the Britain with whom it was his dearest wish that America, his America, should walk in closest association was a Britain equally true to her long and noble tradition of statesmanship and bearing witness, in every fresh generation of her sons, at home and overseas, to the qualities of mind and soul, the valour and endurance and integrity, which have caused her cliff-set, misty island to be regarded as a school of public affairs for all mankind.

# VII

## POLITICS AS AN IDEALISTIC CAREER[1]

THE tradition that the Christian ministry was the most natural activity for a young man who wished to devote his life single-mindedly to the service of his fellows long survived the breakdown of the mediæval system with its dualism between the cloister and the world. But within the last few generations one opening after another has been found through which those who were unwilling to adopt a definitely religious vocation have been able to render service in a similar spirit. The most notable instance is, of course, the profession of teaching. Another is, or was until recently, the profession of journalism. In the nineteenth century the journalist regarded the editorial desk as a pulpit, and however much Matthew Arnold and others have poked fun at the "young lions" of Fleet Street, at least these thought of themselves, and men thought of them, as placed in a position of public service. To-day, the commercialization of the press has largely closed this avenue. There remains one important field in which idealistic effort can—and should—find increasing scope: that of politics.

It is not the object of this essay to discuss politics in general, or this or that political creed in particular, as a substitute for personal religion. Strictly speaking, the very idea of such a substitute is an absurdity; for any interest which dominates a man's thought and action becomes thereby, in the true sense of the word, his religion. If, in

[1]Contributed to the World Committee of the Young Men's Christian Associations.

the present-day world churches are often empty and men's minds and conversation are engrossed by material interests, to which even the churches themselves devote considerable attention, it would surely be more correct to say that money is the religion of to-day than to describe it as a substitute for religion.

How far politics, in their turn, have become, or remained, a religion, it is difficult to say. It might seem at first sight as though the war, and all the devotion and sacrifice it called forth, proved that the political religion —one might almost say the tribal religion—was overwhelmingly strong in the modern world. Thousands and tens of thousands among the combatants, even perhaps millions, when asked why they were offering their lives would have replied "For England," "For France," "For Germany," as the case may be; and there have been not a few thinkers who have taken this as a proof of the power over men's minds of influences wholly disconnected from personal religion and morality. But on closer analysis this conclusion would not seem to be borne out. No doubt there were among those who prepared themselves for the supreme sacrifice a certain number whose outlook was purely tribal; but they were certainly very much in the minority. A far greater number had a vision, however dim and confused, of the political conflict as somehow bound up with moral and religious issues of far more than local or national import. Only so can we explain the psychological development in the later part of the war and, in particular, the immense, if shortlived popularity of President Wilson.

However this may be, it is well to lay down at the outset that, in so far as politics operate as a religious force in the present-day world, the resulting religion is narrowing and retrograde. Politics are not an end in themselves but a means towards a larger end, which is to set the individual free to live his or her own life in society. To concentrate on public affairs the passion and the romance which in their own proper realm produce art, literature, and the other fruits of the spirit is a wasteful diversion of spiritual energy. No one knows this better than those whose work lies in the political field; for they are constantly witnessing Niagaras of idealism running to waste through lack of proper direction—lack, that is, of a trained sense of the scope and limitations of political action. One of the saddest features of the post-war world is the disillusionment of those who, in 1918, were led through confused thinking into entertaining almost Messianic expectations, to the lasting impairment of their moral and mental balance. Well do I remember how in December 1918, when too many of the clergy were lending encouragement to such illusions from the pulpit, one of the leading advocates of the then embryo League of Nations besought those in high place to moderate their ardour; and he did so in the truest interests of religion since, as he argued with cogency, if the churches led the people to expect the Foreign Offices or the Peace Conference to produce an instalment of the millennium they would be laying up in store a disillusionment which could not but be damaging to the religious life of the nation.

What we are concerned with in these pages then is not the kind of politics which seize hold of the mind like a religious revival, unbalance the judgment and obscure the vision of all outside a narrow range. On the contrary, it is the political activity which is diametrically opposed to this type of obsession—the steady and persistent effort of those who have their own sure personal standards of belief and are seeking to apply them to a subject-matter of peculiar importance and complexity.

We leave out of account then the various present-day movements, in so far as they partake of the character of obsessions or religions, and limit ourselves to the fields of public activity open to those who are willing to bring to politics the same kind of conscientious study and application as are looked for in other recognized professions such as medicine, law, teaching, and the higher journalism.

What are those fields?

Political activity, in the strict sense of the term, can be grouped under two main heads, administration and legislation, or, in other words, the work of the Civil Service and the work of a Member of Parliament and of other elected persons.

The Civil Servant is not usually regarded either as a legislator or a politician. But, in fact, to-day, he is both, and his importance in either capacity is rapidly, and even alarmingly, increasing.

A legislator is a person who frames laws. A politician is a person who wields political influence. The Civil Servant of to-day both frames laws, or rather bills, and wields influence, for the simple reason that he, and very often he alone, is in possession of the relevant knowledge.

This is due to a fact to which students of the art of government, and young men considering the chance of a career, cannot pay too much attention—the change in the character of public affairs. A generation or two ago "politics," complicated as they may have seemed to a Peel or a Gladstone, were confined within a comparatively narrow range. The prevailing theory was that of *laissez-faire* and it was only by degrees that social problems in general secured the attention of Parliaments and Government Departments. To-day it is almost universally admitted that the State cannot ignore the wider issues of society, and subjects like health, transport, child-welfare, the traffic in dangerous drugs are not only dealt with nationally but internationally. The result is that a vast amount of technical knowledge is now required in the work of government departments. The Minister himself is less and less able to supervise the details of what is done in his office, and more and more power falls into the hands of the Civil Servants. Moreover, their activities are becoming international, as well as national. There is hardly a British Government Department which has not been represented at some League of Nations conference in recent years and not a few national Civil Servants, men like Sir Hubert Llewellyn Smith, Sir Malcolm Delevingne, Mr. Humbert Wolfe—to mention only British names—are figures almost as well known in Geneva as in Whitehall. We are in fact witnessing the rapid formation of a very powerful bureaucracy, operating on the international plane. As a high authority remarked recently, "we are coming to be governed by a Civil Prætorian Guard."

Our new Prætorians have acquired this power because they have the necessary knowledge and have perfected the necessary technique. But knowledge and method by themselves are not enough. A third element is indispensable—that indefinable element which we call Character.

It is not too much to say that the future of civilization depends upon the League of Nations, the future of the League of Nations upon its technical Committees, and the future of these Committees upon the character of their *personnel*. Everyone who knows administrative offices and the work of Committees from the inside knows the importance of Character. The "personal element," which is nothing on paper, is everything in reality. There is no finer field for the political idealist than in the day-by-day work of applying sound habits and worthy standards in all these regions of technical activity. Truthfulness, honesty, patience, tolerance, disinterestedness are perhaps humdrum virtues: but they are never seen to better advantage, or more genuinely appreciated, than round a Committee table, and most of all when the Committee is of an international character.

There is no royal road to a political career of this kind. Men who have trained themselves to be doctors or bankers, or engineers, or railway experts, or even teachers, may find themselves, before many years are past, in the very centre of politics—in the very thick of the play and interplay of national interests and national character which constitute public affairs in the post-war world.

Let us now turn to the other great branch of political activity, the work of representation.

The task of a representative, particularly of a national representative, in the conditions of present-day democracy, is one of the most delicate and responsible, as well as one of the most interesting, that can be imagined. No career is more worthy to inspire idealistic effort. It is customary to speak of the decline of Parliaments and it is even the fashion in some quarters to point the finger of scorn at Congressmen and members of other representative bodies. And it is indeed the case, as has already been remarked, that these so-called legislators do very little lawmaking to-day. It is seldom that they frame bills themselves and it is not even very common for them to initiate policy. In the growing complexity of public affairs a representative of the general interests of the community cannot possibly possess the special knowledge needed for drawing up policies, still less projects of law, on detailed issues.

But this is not to say that the importance of his function has diminished. All that has happened is that it has changed; and when the change has been realized it will be seen that the Parliamentarian (not to speak of the municipal councillor) has duties which are more, and not less, responsible under the new dispensation than under the old.

What are those duties? They are two-fold—a duty of supervision and a duty of education and interpretation. The modern world is torn asunder by the forces making for specialization. Look where we will, we see the immense power and ever more rapid growth of influences and organizations of a sectional character. Sometimes it is a case of special material interests; practically the whole world of business is run on this basis. But the tendency is equally marked in regions unaffected by considerations of material gain. The natural sciences and the humanities tend to specialize their devotees almost to the same degree as business. To keep abreast of the advance of knowledge in his own study means, for the scholar, a renunciation of many other interests, and too often, amongst the interests thus sacrificed, is included a general concern for the affairs of the community and of the world as a whole. It is the prime duty of a representative to correct this tendency, to keep a constant eye upon the larger issues of the day, on the general interests of his country and their interdependence with world-wide movements and forces. It is his duty to do this, firstly because this is the traditional function of Parliament, at least under the British constitution; and secondly, because, if he and his colleagues do not do so, nobody else will do it for them. There is no other responsible authority in the community which can relieve Parliament of this task. No doubt the University can make a contribution to it in its own field, and so can the various national and international professional organizations. But the general supervision, the final judgment, and the constitutional responsibility rest with the elected representatives of the people. If Parliaments can rise to this responsibility, democracy can be made a reality. In so far as they fail to do so, it will remain, what it is in most of the countries that boast of democratic forms of government to-day, a mere paper scheme, a screen behind which economic or social or administrative groups are the real depositories of power.

But it is not only the duty of a representative to supervise; he must also represent. He is the link between the centre of political activity and the circumference, between the technical expert and the man in the street. He is not a mere delegate. Parliamentary government would quickly break down if representatives arrived in their assemblies bound hand and foot by pledges given to electors in remote localities. Nevertheless a representative cannot ignore local opinion; it is his duty to keep in touch with it, to understand it and to inform it. He is perhaps best described as an interpreter. He interprets the plain man to the expert, the provinces to the metropolis, and vice versa. He is the embodiment of that broad view, sane judgment, and wide general information which, before the days of encroaching specialism, ranked as the hall-mark of an educated man.

But he must be more than educated: he must be an educator. If politics have become complicated and technical, it is for the representative to explain them to the people and to bring out the broad underlying issues on which the electorate is called to judge. And in order to do this he must have established a relationship of confidence between himself and his constituents. That confidence, it is not too much to say, is the most crucial element in the working of the democratic system to-day. And it is given, or withheld, not according to the ability, or eloquence, or even the Parliamentary diligence of the representative, but pre-eminently according to his character. Either the people trust or they mistrust. Once they give their trust, they allow their representative great latitude. Once they withdraw their trust from a public man, even if he can still win elections, his career is morally ended. Here again, as round the committee table, character is all-decisive. The desirability of maintaining conditions which facilitate the establishment of such relations of confidence is one of the prime considerations to be borne in mind in the discussion of electoral systems and methods. This is too complicated a subject to be gone into here; but the failure to remember this has certainly been a disadvantage in the working of proportional representation, at least in some of its less carefully considered forms.

How can a young man prepare himself for work of this character? Is the function of being an elected person in itself a career?

To ask these questions is to open up one of the most important subjects of discussion in connexion with the working of democratic institutions. It is a subject which has been too long evaded. This is not the place in which to go into it in detail. Suffice it to say that, whatever view is held as to the desirability of regarding Parliamentary life as a definite career for a young man, it is certainly, under present conditions, a whole-time occupation. Those who are chosen for it should give their whole time to it and should receive a sufficient salary to render them relatively immune from the temptations inseparable from their position. Here again we come back to the element of Character.

Finally, leaving the field of politics as a special occupation, a word must be said about the general duty of citizenship under the conditions of to-day.

The democratic system is based on the assumption that in a civilized community the ordinary citizen is interested in public affairs from the standpoint of the public interest. Is this a valid assumption to-day? In some countries with advanced constitutions it is evidently not and we therefore see public affairs being treated simply as a football for contending private interests. Even in the countries which have hitherto worked democratic constitutions with fair success (the reader can find the list of them, as Bryce judged them in 1914, in his book on *Modern Democracies*), there have since the war been ominous signs of a decline in two directions. The ordinary voter is less interested in politics than he was; and, concurrently and partly as a consequence, private interests are more and more asserting their influence in the public domain. If this process continues unchecked it will be fatal, not simply to democracy, but to the art of Government itself. Government is the management of public affairs. But when men no longer feel that there *are* public affairs, when the common interest (*res publica*, in the old Roman phrase) is broken up into atoms of sectional interest, government as such comes to an end and politics become simply a special branch of private business.

To counteract this tendency, to affirm the dignity of public affairs and the responsibility of the citizen for dealing with them is not only a political necessity, but a moral duty—at the present juncture of world affairs one of the most pressing of moral duties. And those who are attempting to discharge it need all the reinforcement that can be provided by the idealism of the younger generation.

# VIII

## GREAT BRITAIN, THE DOMINIONS, AND THE LEAGUE OF NATIONS[1]

JUST at the moment when the French newspapers were recording the results of the elections to the Chamber of Deputies at Paris in Algiers and Cochin China, Martinique and Senegal, the British press was recording an item that passed practically unnoticed in France—the appointment of a High Commissioner of Great Britain to the Canadian government at Ottawa, the first appointment of a diplomatic character made from London in a Dominion capital.

The French colonial elections were manifestations of a long and firmly-rooted tradition of centralization. The British appointment was the culmination of an equally long and firmly-rooted tradition of decentralization.

Englishmen, confronted at first sight with the French system, are apt to ask themselves, and their French friends, whether assimilation and centralization do not conceal an imperceptible process of tyranny and extinction of vital values. Equally, Frenchmen, confronted with the British system, are inclined to ask whether decentralization is not simply a graceful synonym for total disintegration.

The French answer to the English questioning must be given for English readers. Here the effort will be made to explain to French readers why, in spite, and indeed just because, of the progress of formal symptoms of disintegration, the British Empire not only survives in undiminished

[1] Contributed to *L'Année Politique française et étrangère*, 1928.

strength but has actually increased its fitness to cope with the problems of the post-war world.

The exposition that follows divides itself naturally into three parts. First it is necessary to trace the historical development of the existing system. Next will come an analysis of the present situation and policy of the Empire. Finally, having watched the new institutions in operation, we shall consider their significance from a more general point of view, as interesting to students of political science.

No one can understand the present relationship of the Dominions to Great Britain if he has not constantly present in his mind the fundamental conditions of British political life.

The British Empire is outwardly fragile, but, in its essence, extremely solid. In this it resembles the political power in Great Britain itself. *"Ce serait le destin de la puissance exécutrice,"* said Montesquieu, of Great Britain two hundred years ago, *"d'être presque toujours inquiétée au dedans et respectée au dehors."* He added that *"si quelque puissance étrangère menaçait l'Etat et le mettait en danger de sa fortune et de sa gloire, les petits intérêts cèderaient aux plus grands, tout se réunirait en faveur de la puissance exécutrice."* These last words were signally verified in 1914 and, in spite of the constitutional developments since that date—and even because of them—it is safe to prophesy that they will be verified again. In the same way, government in Great Britain itself, so much weaker in appearance than that of countries with more rigid laws and a stronger central administration, is stronger than ever in an age which has not only passed through the experience of a general strike but is witnessing a steady process of the devolution of responsibility to local and professional bodies. It is sufficient to cite two facts, each typical in their domain. During the general strike a cricket match took place in a large centre of population between a team of policemen and a team of strikers. It was symbolic of the spirit in which their larger contest was being conducted. In the sphere of local government, the "Board" or Ministry of Education which is steadily relaxing its hold over the details of the administration by the local education authorities, has no power to insert, or to exclude, a subject from the time-table. Thus, in order to ensure that patriotism, or the League of Nations, should be universally taught in the state-supported English schools, it is necessary to convince, individually, each of some 300 local authorities. To this, it is worth while adding a third observation—that, in point of fact, patriotism is not taught, as a regular subject, in English schools and that about a million Englishmen freely volunteered to serve in the Great War. It is in the light of facts such as these, and of the underlying conditions which make them possible, that the study of the organisation, or want of organisation, of the Third, or post-war, British Empire must be approached.

Some years ago the writer of these lines had the privilege of a conversation with the Premier of Canada upon the constitutional problems of the British Empire. Mr. Mackenzie King, himself the grandson of the leader of a rebellion against authority exercised from London, had been setting forth his familiar thesis of the equality of status between Great Britain and the Dominions. "Come upstairs," he said, at the conclusion of his argument, "and I will prove you my case from the highest authority." We ascended to the library where he produced a gramophone and in a few moments we were listening to a speech delivered at the Empire Exhibition at Wembley by His

Majesty King George V which specifically confirmed the Canadian Premier's thesis.

This incident may serve as a fitting introduction to a brief summary of the evolution of Dominion status: for the story begins, as it ends, with the assertion of a special relationship to the Crown over the head of the Parliament and Ministry of Great Britain. No doubt "the Crown" which gave Royal Charters to the early seventeenth century colonists differs as greatly, in the constitutional domain, from "the Crown" in 1928 as James I and Charles I differ in personal qualities and outlook from George V. In that constitutional difference indeed lies the whole essence of the development. Nevertheless the continuity of the name, the function and the dynasty is symbolic of the continuity of a sentiment and a tradition which are among the most binding elements in the British Empire of to-day. When the Imperial Conference of 1926 agreed that full powers for signing a treaty affecting an individual Dominion should be given by his Majesty to the person designated by the government of that Dominion without a counter-signature by a representative of the London government, it was deciding in favour of the King's subjects overseas a controversy dating from the seventeenth century. Had the colonists who rebelled against London in the eighteenth century only had King George III to deal with, they would never have drawn up the Declaration of Independence. Despite their assumption of republican ideas, which fitted them as ill as Marxian ideas fit the British Labour man of to-day, their real quarrel was not with the dynasty but with the Parliament. "The Americans, going on precedents prior to the Revolution of 1688," writes the latest historian of England,[1]

[1] G. M. Trevelyan: *History of England*, 1926, p. 550.

"distinguished sharply between the Crown, whose authority they admitted within limits, and the Westminster
Parliament, which they regarded as a local assembly. To
the English this distinction was impossible because the
'Crown in Parliament' was for them the supreme authority."

These words, written of the contending views at the
time of the American War of Independence, still hold
good to-day. The Canadian Premier, listening to the
Wembley gramophone record, acknowledges the authority of the Crown *within limits* and His Majesty's government in Great Britain, as it is now officially called, still
regards "The Crown in Parliament" as the supreme
authority. There is an element of unsolved controversy
here to which we shall return. For the moment it is enough
to emphasize the fact that Mr. Mackenzie King is as loyal
to the Crown as George Washington was before a foolish
ministry drove him to extremes, and that London in 1926
placed itself in the impossibility of repeating the mistaken
policy which led to 1776.

Why is the grandson of William Lyon Mackenzie, the
rebel, content, and indeed proud, to be the minister of
George V? Why is Canada, why are Ireland and South
Africa, content to remain in the British Empire? These
are natural questions to be put by those who, like most
Frenchmen, have been brought up to regard republican
institutions and sovereign national independence as two
of the highest political goods. And if there is a minority
of Irishmen and South Africans who are asking the same
questions it is chiefly because they have been subject to
the same Continental intellectual influences. But the
majority of the citizens of the Dominions do not so frame
the question. Where the Frenchman says *why*, they say,

quite simply, *why not?* That *why not* embodies not simply the continued existence, the *vis inertiæ*, but also the continuing power and momentum of the British Empire. Why not, say the subjects of King George, if membership of the British Empire helps to give us the conditions that we need.

Englishmen do not regard politics as an end in themselves. They are not Utopians. They do not dream of the British Empire as an instalment of the perfect state. They do not feel for it the mystical reverence which Continental Socialists have evoked for the Socialist State of the future and which misplaced sentimentalists have poured out on the League of Nations. They regard it with respect and a certain intimate affection as an admirable instrument for fulfilling certain practical objects and so long as it continues to fulfil these objects they will continue to answer the Continental critic's Why? with a Why not? Those practical objects form the "limits" of the loyalty to which the British historian cited above refers.

What are those objects? What does an Englishman, and an overseas Briton formed on the English tradition, expect from his political institutions?

To answer this question is to trace the course of British constitutional history; for what Englishmen value to-day in their political institutions is what they have won for themselves, and embodied in them, in the past: and they continue to value them in the order of their attainment. What was needed most, and won first, is still valued most to-day.

British political institutions, when analysed, are found to consist of three strata superimposed one upon the other.

The oldest and deepest stratum is that of individual liberty and personal rights. England is the mother of the

freedom of the person. Guaranteed to-day by the Habeas
Corpus Act of 1679, it was believed by the men of that
generation to go back to the Magna Charta of 1215. We
need not enquire into these historical origins. Suffice it to
say that for centuries past, in every rank of English society,
the respect for individual liberty, and the determination
to prevent its abridgement by executive or legislative action
has been the strongest force in English public life. It has
been so strong that, like the British navy in the nineteenth
century, it has seldom needed to show its strength. But,
at the least hint of danger, as in a recent case of abuse of
powers by the police, the authorities find themselves
faced with a unanimous and deeply stirred public opinion.
Perhaps the best way of realising the place which respect
for personal liberty holds in the English political system
and in that of the Dominions which are loyal to it is to
observe how, when local conditions, as in South Africa,
are unfavourable to its strict observance, the whole spirit
of the system is affected and what can only be called an
"un-British" atmosphere is brought into being. This is not
the place in which to test the Colour Bar legislation of the
South African government by the principles of the British
Constitution. But if the hoisting of the new South African
flag on May 31 last led to hostile manifestations by the
natives, this is an indication of how easily a government
can transgress the limits set by expediency and turn the
minds of citizens used to the traditions of British rule from
a contented "why not" to a critical and even indignant
"why"? The crowd at Pretoria was manifesting against
the Dominion Government, not against London which has
more consistently safeguarded native liberties. But it is
not difficult to imagine hypothetical circumstances under
which similar manifestations in the name of personal

liberty and self-respect might be made against London. Any government foolish enough to provoke such a sentiment would have taken the surest road to the disintegration of the Empire.

Inseparably bound up with the idea of individual liberty are the elementary civil rights—freedom of speech and worship, freedom of meeting and of association. They are so completely ingrained in the texture of English life and the English tradition that it is hard for Englishmen to realise how recent is the French legislation favouring the growth of voluntary associations within the state and harder still to understand how the citizens of a country of old civilisation, like Italy, can allow such rights to be withdrawn from them without effective resistance.

In his remarkable book *Au delà du Marxisme*[1] Henri de Man makes a penetrating analysis of the inferiority complex of the European working man as one of the main psychological elements in the Socialist movement. "*Parmi les modifications que la vie sociale apporte aux tendances instinctives, inhérentes à l'organisation physiologique de l'homme,*" he writes, "*il n'en est pas de plus importante que la coloration de tous les instincts animaux par l'instinct d'autovaluation. Cette expression,*" he continues, "*me parait le meilleur équivalent de ce que la psychologie anglo-saxonne, représentée par McDougall, appelle l'instinct de self-assertion, ce qui correspond à peu près au 'Geltungstrieb' allemand, et ressemble par certains côtés à ce que la langue française appelle l'amour propre, pas assez complètement cependant pour que l'on puisse se contenter de cette expression courante et faire ainsi l'économie d'un vocable nouveau.*"

The degree in which this instinct is satisfied for the ordinary British citizen through the traditional laws, customs and

[1]Brussels, 1926, p. 45.

policies under the unwritten British constitution is a powerful element in the contentment, the Why not psychology, which characterises the British political world to-day. It helps to explain not only why the British working man believes in co-operation rather than class-war and in evolution rather than revolution, but why Canada and Australia, countries which owe their very existence to the initiative, will-power and self-respect of their settlers, nevertheless find sufficient satisfaction for this self-respect inside the British Empire.

The second element in the British political tradition is Parliamentary Government. The King's Courts of Justice were in regular working order at least a century before the establishment of Parliament. Nevertheless the House of Commons is rightly called the Mother of Parliaments and England is the great source of the parliamentary tradition. True, the House of Commons in the early seventeenth century, before the victory of the Parliament over the King in the Civil War, had not the prestige and authority which it acquired a few generations later. Nevertheless to the early settlers an Assembly was almost as much a necessity of social existence as the safeguarding of personal rights. And once the seed of Parliament was planted, the victory of the representatives of the electors over the executive was as inevitable in the overseas colonies as in England itself—more inevitable in fact, since it is more natural for a legislature to insist on its rights against a power at a distance than against one close at hand. It is true that after the loss of the American colonies the London government attempted for two generations to arrest the growth of Parliamentary government in Canada. The result was rebellion, and in 1839 the famous Report of Lord Durham conceded for Colonial parliaments the victory against the executive that had been won in England in the seventeenth century. In the three or four generations that have since elapsed there has been a steady growth not in the nature but in the range of the power exerted by what are now called Dominion Parliaments. How rapid this growth has been, and how quickly the minds of Englishmen have become adapted to it, is best shown by one example. In 1910 Mr. Amery, who at present holds the double office of Secretary of State for the Dominions and Secretary of State for the Colonies, speaking to a students' club at Oxford, on the theme of "imperial unity" said: "The control of foreign policy in fact means, not only the right to conduct specific negotiations on points of detail, but inevitably carries with it, in the long run, the power of making treaties and alliances, and an uncontrolled decision over the issue of peace and war. Once these powers are no longer exercised in common, the Empire for all practical purposes has ceased to exist."[1] Only twelve years later, in September, 1922, the Government of Great Britain appealed to the Dominion governments for help in contemplated military and naval operations against Turkey which involved, in fact if not in name, a declaration of war against that country. The Canadian Premier replied that he could take no decision without consulting the Canadian Parliament. The Chanak crisis marks the end of the long evolution through which the early colonial assemblies developed into bodies co-equal with the Mother of Parliaments in what Mr. Amery recognised in 1910 to be the crucial power of peace and war.

A well-known French statesman and professor, speaking of the rights accorded by Great Britain to the Dominions, remarked recently that he did not know whether they had

[1] *Union and Strength*, by L. S. Amery, London, 1912, p. 6.

been granted willingly and out of principle or simply
"*pour faire bonne mine au mauvais jeu*," but that in any
case Frenchmen could rest assured that no such surrender
of power to the overseas French colonial communities
would be made in Paris. His attitude on this subject to-day
is psychologically identical with that of Mr. Amery in
1910, when he declared that such a surrender would mean
that the Empire for all practical purposes would cease to
exist. Nevertheless the powers have been surrendered in
London with the complete and almost enthusiastic assent
of the English people, and the British Empire not only
continues to exist but is apparently stronger than ever. Is
it not possible that Mr. Amery in 1910 and his French
colleague in 1928 were not sufficiently supple in their
thinking, that they forgot that constitutions were made
for human beings and not human beings for constitutions?

How is it possible, in fact, for the Canadian Parliament
to have secured the right to make peace and war and for
the Canadian Government and people to remain whole-
heartedly loyal to the British Empire?

The answer can only be given in psychological terms.

Englishmen overseas have always considered that they
have a right to the same institutions as Englishmen in
England. They have even carried this to the point of
meticulous imitation in matters of form and ceremonial.
Their very attachment to English institutions led them to
desire to reproduce them on colonial soil.

Moreover, by a strange phenomenon of unconscious
cultural imperialism, they have succeeded in inoculating
non-English populations under the British flag with the
same craving. Theoretically according to the traditional
philosophy of the British constitution, English liberty
and English parliamentary institutions were a hereditary

personal right of Englishmen. But when after 1763 a mere
handful of Englishmen found themselves living under the
British flag in Canada among a population of 60,000
French, English common sense—not to speak of elementary prudence—forbade the attempt to confine the privileges of the English tradition to an insignificant minority.
Hence it came about that in 1791 Parliamentary institutions on the traditional English model were granted to the
French in Quebec on the same terms as to the English in
the adjoining province. From this time forward Parliamentarism ceased to be *"jus sanguinis,"* a right of Englishmen as Englishmen, and became *"jus soli,"* a right of all
subjects of His Majesty who have attained to the necessary degree of responsibility for its exercise. It is the Act
of 1791 which decided once and for all, that what we know
to-day as the British Empire should not be simply an
English Empire. What was granted to Quebec in 1791 was
granted to the provinces of South Africa in 1906 and to a
United South Africa in 1909. It has been granted also, in
incomplete form, it is true, to the central and provincial
assemblies of India, elected by that small proportion of
the Indian population to whom hitherto the franchise has
been granted.

Thus it has come about that such central government
as the British Empire possesses to-day consists, not in a
single authority issuing commands from London, but in a
Conference of Prime Ministers each responsible to their
respective Parliaments, and that, incredible though it may
seem to some French minds, this system works because it
corresponds to the psychological conditions.

The Imperial Conference—as it has been called since
1907—may indeed seem a fragile bond. It meets but once
every four years. The Foreign Ministers of the Little

Entente meet together eight times as often and the Foreign Ministers and other government delegates of the fourteen States comprising the Council of the League of Nations meet sixteen times as often. By a strange irony the Conference system planned in 1919 for the League of Nations on the model of the Imperial Conference has developed far more rapidly than its prototype, so that, whereas the Imperial Conference brings the representatives of Great Britain and the Dominions together once every four years, the Assembly brings them to Geneva every year and the Council, since the elections of 1927, brings Canada and Great Britain together every quarter. We shall leave aside for the moment the reasons for this apparently paradoxical discrepancy. Suffice it to say that it denotes no weakening of the imperial tie and that the system of Parliamentary self-government adopted in the Dominions on the English model made no other kind of central organisation practicable. An Imperial Parliament is indeed theoretically conceivable: but it runs counter to the whole psychological development. The representatives of the Dominions are no more willing to submit to being outvoted, and accepting majority decisions, than are the sovereign states represented at Geneva. Thus the Empire, like the League of Nations, arrives at agreed decisions only through the unanimity of the Parliaments of its constituent Dominions.

The third stratum in the English political system is democracy. With one exception, the Parliaments of the Dominions are elected, like that of Great Britain, by the great majority of the people. Moreover the power thus placed in the hands of the people is really exercised. Public opinion (which is not to be confused with newspaper opinion) is a force to be reckoned with, as every member of Parliament knows. The British peoples are politically minded. They take a close interest in public affairs and enjoy using their judgment upon political questions. The one Dominion which is not democratic is South Africa, where the majority of the population, being non-white, is almost entirely excluded from the franchise and Parliamentary government rests upon an oligarchical, rather than a democratic, basis.

The South African system serves as a reminder that democracy is a comparatively new force in British political life. Personal rights and parliamentary government were not built up by the people; they were secured under a system of minority rule. They were achieved for the people but not by the people. It must never be forgotten in studying British institutions, in contrast with those of the United States and the Continent, that they are not based on the theory of the sovereignty of the people, or on a revolutionary victory of the many over the few. They are based on the principle of the civil rights of individual Englishmen and on the slow extension of political responsibility, and of the customs and habits of mind engendered by it, to an ever-widening circle. From this point of view England is not so much a democracy as an aristocracy with a marvellous power of assimilating plebeian elements; and, in the social sphere, this is only too evident, even in a generation which has seen a Labour government in office. But this aristocracy has throughout the centuries been devoted to the rule of law. In spite of the fact that there is no written constitution—or indeed, just because of that fact—the truest political adjective which can be applied to England is "constitutional." England is a constitutional country and the individual Englishman is by nature, training and inclination, constitutionally minded.

This was never so clearly demonstrated as during the general strike, when the so-called revolutionists seemed intent on showing how little revolutionary they were.

Let us now sum up this theoretical prelude to the analysis of the present situation.

The British Empire consists of a number of communities possessing a political system modelled on that of England. The main elements of this system are civil liberty, parliamentary government and the rule of public opinion through the ballot-box. The natural result of its working has been to relax the constitutional bonds between the metropolis and the overseas "colonies" and "possessions," as they used to be called, and to bring into existence a number of independent self-reliant states taking a pride in managing their own affairs. British constitutionalism, in other words, produces a constitutional habit of mind in individual British citizens, but at the same time operates against the establishment of a constitutional tie between the States of which they are members.

This impression of decentralisation, not to speak of disintegration, is strengthened when one turns from history and constitutional theory to an analysis of the facts and forces of the present day.

Examine closely on the map the extent and composition of the British Empire.

It numbers one quarter of the inhabitants of the world, a somewhat larger figure than China. But whereas China is homogeneous, the British Empire is the most heterogeneous political entity that can be conceived, and it is becoming more heterogeneous every day.

Portions of it are to be found in every one of the five Continents, or seven if we divide America into North,

Central and South. And the communities thus separated
on the map present every variety of climate, of natural
resources, of race, religion, culture and stage of development. Age-old civilisations like those of India and of the
Chinese in Hong-Kong and the Kowloon and Wei-hai-Wei
territories are side by side with the young institutions of
the settlers in New Zealand and Western Canada and the
primitive and hardly yet adolescent races of Africa. What
common interest, it may be asked, holds together the
wheat farmers of Western Canada, the Chinese traders of
Hong-Kong, the sugar planters of Mauritius, the peasant
cultivators of India, the sheep farmers of Australia and
New Zealand and the industrial working men of Great
Britain? They have certain common political institutions.
But these institutions, by their very nature, are drawing
them apart. Can economic interests bring together what
political influences seem to be drawing asunder? Incapable
of being made into a political unit, according to the old
conceptions of political unity, can the British Empire be
made into an economic unit?

The idea of imperial economic unity has been a dream
of a certain school of English statesmanship for many
generations; but events have proved that it is even more
unrealisable than political centralisation. For political independence implies also necessarily independence in economic policy, and the first use that the Dominions have
made of their independence in economic policy has been to
erect tariffs on goods from foreign countries, including
Great Britain. The loud propaganda in favour of imperial
preference which still goes on should not blind continental
observers to the fact that after some fifty years of effort
practically nothing has been achieved. A real preferential
system between Great Britain and the overseas British

communities is indeed impossible, as a moment's reflection will show. What does the British elector need in the economic sphere? Cheap food and cheap raw materials. What have the overseas British communities to sell to him? Chiefly foodstuffs and raw materials—the wheat of Canada, the meat and wood of Australia and of New Zealand. What is their interest? To get the best possible price. Are the Canadian wheat farmers and the Australian pastoralists going to lower their price for the benefit of the English consumer or manufacturer, or is the English housewife willing to pay more for her bread and her meat in order to gratify her fellow-citizens overseas? The answer has already been given in numerous elections and it is now accepted by all parties in England that a true system of preference, applied to the leading products of the Dominions, is outside the realm of practical politics. Attempts are still being made to develop systems of exclusive trading in the non-self-governing Empire, but it is only a question of time before the same logic of self-interest works itself out in that region also. The cocoa growers of the Gold Coast and the cotton growers of the Sudan will not reserve their products for the English market if they can get a better price elsewhere.

We are driven therefore to the conclusion that there are, broadly speaking, no *special material interests* common to the countries of the British Empire. By special interests is meant interests shared by them all but not shared by other territories. And if this is true of material interests it is also true of cultural or intellectual interests. There is no British type of culture and no British type of education. It is not possible to regard any one centre, London, for instance, or Oxford, as the intellectual metropolis of the Empire. If Cecil Rhodes indulged in such a dream a generation ago events have shown that it must remain a dream. The British Empire does not consist, like the Roman, of a capital at the centre surrounded by provinces at the circumference, but of a number of living centres, each engaged in developing their own characteristic form of national life and culture.

This is the explanation of the phenomenon we have already noted—the failure of the Imperial Conference to bring into existence any imperial institutions worthy of the name. The League of Nations has only existed since 1920. It consists of over fifty States exhibiting the same heterogeneity, only over a far wider area, as the countries of the British Empire. Its decisions are equally taken by unanimity and it would be expected that such unanimity would be more difficult to secure. Nevertheless the League of Nations has succeeded in bringing into existence in eight years a series of technical organisations very much more numerous and important, and covering a far wider range, than the meagre products of the Imperial Conference.[1] The reason for this striking discrepancy is very simple. It is not that the peoples of the British Empire do not wish to co-operate. It is that there is nothing particular for them to co-operate together about. Or, to be more strictly accurate, there are very few subjects which form a natural basis for official co-operation—co-operation between Governments. Voluntary co-operation there is in plenty and will always continue to be, whether the Empire remains in being or whether it disintegrates. But the absence of special official organizations of co-operation between the governments of the British Empire is due to

---

[1] The French reader will find a brief account of the latter on pp. 172-4 of "l'Empire Britannique," by H. Demangeon, published in 1923. There have been a few additions since, notably the "Imperial Economic Committee," but the position remains substantially the same.

the simple fact that the common interests of those governments and their peoples are not particular to themselves
but common to all or most other peoples. In other words,
they are international. It follows that the most convenient
organisations for co-operation in regard to them will not
be imperial but international. What these general interests
are we will see later. Here we will merely note that we have
arrived at the explanation why Great Britain and Canada
meet four times a year at Geneva and only once in four
years in London. They have at least sixteen times as many
problems of common interest to discuss together at Geneva
as in London.

Not only are there few or no special common interests
between the peoples of the Empire, but their separate
interests are showing a tendency to become more and more
divergent. In the nineteenth century it was not difficult
for the London government to conduct a foreign policy
that was agreeable to the people of Canada and the people
of Australia. But with the growth of the Dominions and
the development of an articulate national public opinion,
agreement becomes much more difficult. Democracy is
often declared to be a power for peace. In a broad sense
this is true and much can be done to make better use of the
genuine goodwill which animates the ordinary voter, be
he peasant or working man or shopkeeper. Nevertheless,
in any particular controversy, democracies are apt, if not
to be bellicose, at least to stand very stiffly upon what they
consider their rights—and not only their rights but their
interests. Thus the increased power of public opinion in the
various countries of the British Empire is making the
maintenance of a common British foreign policy increasingly difficult. One instance will be sufficient to make this
plain. In 1921, when the Anglo-Japanese alliance was due

to expire, most of the members of the Imperial Conference of that year wished it to be renewed. Canada, whose opinion on foreign affairs is always largely influenced by the United States, did not. The dilemma thus presented to the London Government was only solved by the expedient of the quadrilateral pact adopted at the Washington Conference some months later. But the Empire cannot count on such a *"deus ex machina"* in every difficulty; and in fact the Locarno Agreements provide an instance of a divergence of policy between London and Ottawa which has not yet been bridged over.

This will become clearer if we examine briefly the change that has taken place in the position and interests of Great Britain as a result of the War.

During the century that elapsed between the battle of Trafalgar and July 1914, Great Britain enjoyed a position of predominance so solidly assured that it seldom required to be affirmed by the show of physical force. This predominance was based firstly on a naval supremacy which enabled Great Britain to impose her will by means of a fleet more powerful than that of any two other powers: secondly, on a commercial and industrial supremacy resulting from the fact that she had been the first to profit by the industrial revolution at the end of the eighteenth century, and connected also with her command of coal.

These conditions enabled Great Britain to maintain herself free from entanglements in what was called glorious isolation. Supreme on the oceans, her only concern with the Continent, apart from its value to her as a market, was to ensure that no supremacy arose there which might in time threaten her own power. Thus glorious isolation and the balance of power, however incompatible in theory, went well together in practice: and with them went a third doctrine, also the product of this temporary supremacy, the elimination of commercial barriers.

The War has swept away the means by which Great Britain maintained these policies.

She is no longer supreme at sea. To-day her fleet is equal to that of the United States. To-morrow it may be inferior. Peace is still to her a primary interest: but she is no longer able to impose her will throughout the oceans of the world.

She is no longer supreme in the economic field. Nevertheless, she still lives by foreign trade and needs the elimination of commercial barriers. But there are other powerful wills in the sphere of economic policy to be set against her own.

Moreover, the Continent of Europe, which ever since the end of the Middle Ages had been divided by competing dynasties and where, since 1789, two rival principles had been contending for mastery, is now, if not united, at least showing in many spheres signs of a co-operative organisation which renders the doctrine of the Balance of Power obsolete. What could be achieved by glorious isolation, by the passive use of an unseen but unquestioned supremacy in the nineteenth century can only be secured in the post-War world by a policy of co-operation.

Thus both the development of her own domestic concerns within her own Empire and the movement of events outside it converge towards a policy of co-operation. If co-operation has replaced central control as the accepted system in the relations between Great Britain and the Dominions, it has equally replaced isolation in the relations between Great Britain and other states.

What form of co-operation should Great Britain adopt in these circumstances?

The question has never presented itself to British statesmen in this abstract form. Had it been so presented in 1919, they would doubtless have replied that they would adopt a system of imperial co-operation for the lesser League of Nations comprising the nations of the British Empire and a system of international co-operation for the rest of the world, grouped in the larger League of Nations; and they would probably have added a confident expression of opinion that the lesser League, composed of peoples with a common loyalty and common political ideals would develop more rapidly than the larger. But, being Englishmen, they refrained from speculation, helped to set the larger League going, and waited to see the result.

And the result, as we have seen, is that the larger League has been found to be a more useful agency, even for imperial co-operation, than the smaller. The Geneva League of Nations has, in fact, become an indispensable part of the system of the British Empire.

No doubt the same statement might be made of any and every country which has sincerely subscribed to the Covenant. It is impossible for a Frenchman or a Dane, who reflects on the problems confronting his country, to leave out of account the significant factors which the League of Nations represents for France or Denmark respectively. But it is always possible for a Frenchman or a Dane to think out some other expedient—less satisfactory, no doubt—by which peace and the other national interests safeguarded for his country by the League may be preserved. In the case of Great Britain this is not so. For her the League of Nations is literally indispensable and its weakening or elimination would be a disaster of the first magnitude.

This is seen most clearly in regard to the question of peace and war.

We have seen that the Dominions have secured for themselves the right to decide for themselves the issues of peace and war. We have also seen that their interests are often different from those of Great Britain, separated from most of them by vast spaces of ocean. We have also seen that democracies are both obstinate and short-sighted. In the light of these conditions with what confidence could a British statesman, anxious to maintain the unity of the Empire, face the prospect of a continuance of the system of local wars, such as existed prior to 1914? If the local war is in Europe, Canada and South Africa have indeed already refused to pledge themselves to take part in it. The fact is that the Locarno system of regional pacts and local guarantees, which may be suited to the conditions of certain Continental nations, is quite unsuited to the conditions of the British Empire. The British Empire needs peace everywhere and all the time. It needs a general guarantee of peace as such, irrespective of the geographical and other conditions. It is of small value to those who wish to keep the people of Canada and Australia thinking along the same lines of general policy as the people of Great Britain, to build up an ingenious system of local pacts by which one part of the Empire is defended in this way and another in that way. The British Empire lives by the ocean. The ocean is one and indivisible. The arrangements for the safeguarding of peace should be equally one and indivisible. Thus it may be regarded as certain, despite the rejection of the Geneva Protocol in March 1925, that British public opinion will eventually adopt a universal, rather than a regional, plan for the maintenance of peace. Such a universal plan is, of course, a world interest: but it is also pre-eminently a British interest.

The same reasoning holds good in the field of economic policy. Great Britain is not interested in the breaking down of economic barriers in this or that region. She is interested in the breaking down of economic barriers in every part of the world. Living as she does by foreign trade and dependent upon the ocean paths for her food and raw material, she is more dependent than any other state upon international economic co-operation. And such co-operation, as is now becoming very clear, can best be developed through the activities of the League of Nations, including the International Labour Office. Here again, the observer of British policy should not be misled by ephemeral phases of policy. British governments may have shown reluctance to co-operate in this or that question, such as the Eight Hours Convention and the abolition of import prohibitions. Such incidents are due to special and temporary circumstances. In the long run the broad tendencies of national policy re-assert themselves. "*L'Angleterre est une île marchande; voilà tout le secret de sa politique,*" wrote Albert Sorel of Great Britain at the end of the eighteenth century. The "trading island" of the nineteenth century met its needs through an individualistic system, backed up by the police-force of a supreme navy. The trading island of the twentieth century can only meet them through a co-operative system safeguarded by the League of Nations.

There is another respect, which may be of special interest to French readers, in which the League of Nations helps to maintain the unity of the British Empire. That Empire, as we have seen, comprises all the races of mankind. Of the 440 million human beings who owe allegiance

to King George V, only one in seven is white. The other six
belong to those non-white races who are just painfully
recovering their self-respect after their realisation of the
material power of western civilisation. The British Empire has before it, like that of France, the tremendous task
of transforming a race-ascendency into a partnership. It is
faced in Asia to-day, in Africa to-morrow, with movements
of national self-assertion, similar in kind, but more
intense owing to the special circumstances, to the national
movements which swept through Europe between 1789
and 1918. In a world in which war is still a regular institution, what hope is there that this problem of the relation
between the white and non-white races could be solved in
peace? If nationalism has led to war in almost every
country in Europe from Spain to Finland and from Ireland
to Greece, how should it not lead to war in the infinitely
more complex and inflammable conditions of Asia and
Africa? And if it should lead to war, what hope is there
that the unity of the British Empire could be maintained?
For this problem of the white and the non-whites the British Empire needs the safeguarding of peace by the League,
and the League for its part needs the example and the
moral authority afforded by the *Pax Britannica* which has
hitherto, sometimes, as in the case of India and South
Africa, even in the most unpromising circumstances,
succeeded in preserving not only technical peace but good
relations.

But it may well be asked, at this point, does not your
reasoning over-reach itself? In proving that the British
Empire needs the League of Nations in order to preserve
its own unity, have you not proved too much? If the
Empire can only survive in and through the League, is not
the League taking the place of the Empire, as the Council

and the Assembly and the League's technical Committees are taking the place of the Imperial Conference? Is not your song of triumph over the relief afforded by the League to the Empire in its post-War problems in reality a funeral dirge to commemorate its quiet and painless extinction?

So indeed it would appear to the student of paper constitutions. But to those who look behind technicalities to realities, the situation is very different. Thus to the question: "What remains of the British Empire under the system of international co-operation?" we would answer: "On paper, nothing, or practically nothing; in reality, everything, and more than everything."

"On paper, nothing, or practically nothing." Let us be scrupulously exact. The Imperial Conference Resolutions of 1926, drafted, it is believed, by Lord Balfour and accepted by the Parliaments of all the Dominions, including Great Britain (for under them Great Britain is herself now one of the King's Dominions), defines their position as follows: "They are autonomous Communities within the British Empire, equal in status, in no way subordinate one to another in any aspect of their domestic or external affairs, though united by a common allegiance to the Crown and freely associated as members of the British Commonwealth of Nations." But the Report goes on to add that "the principles of equality and similarity appropriate to status do not universally extend to function; and there are, in fact, so many matters of detail in which the equality conceded in principle has not yet been applied in detail that Professor Keith, the leading authority on the organisation of the British Empire is able to say without injustice, of the definition of Lord Balfour, that it "may be admired for its intention rather than for its

accuracy as a description of fact as opposed to ideal."[1]
Moreover it must always be remembered that the different
Dominions are at very different stages of their political
evolution and that rights claimed and secured by Canada
and the Irish Free State are sometimes regarded as entirely superfluous by New Zealand. For our present purpose, however, the details on which Professor Keith develops with such unwearied learning and, at times, with
such refreshing candour, are of minor interest. It is no
doubt interesting to learn that, although in theory the
Governor-General of a Dominion is no longer the channel
of communication with the London Government, Mr.
Baldwin told the House of Commons on November 25,
1926 that "the position of the Governor-General as to
reservation of Bills had not been dealt with at the Conference and his Imperial functions in this regard would
not be affected." "This negates, of course," as Professor
Keith drily remarks, "his complete supersession as a
channel of correspondence." In the same way Mr. Amery
is still found arguing before an English audience[2] that
"the Crown in the Empire is one and undivided. There was
a time when the King of England was also King of Han-
over, but he was King in two different capacities, the
wearer of two different crowns, and indeed the holder of
crowns having different laws of succession; and so the time
came when the two crowns separated. There is no such
division within the British Empire. The King is not King
of Great Britain in one capacity, King of Australia in
another. He is King in the same sense and capacity as
wearer of the Crown of the whole Empire, and from that
follows one vitally important aspect of the whole Con-

[1] *Responsible Government of the Dominions*, 2nd edition, 1927, Vol. 2, p. 1224.
[2] *Journal of the Royal Institute of International Affairs*, Jan., 1927, p. 16.

stitution, namely, that whatever may be the forms of government, there runs through the whole Empire the common status, the common nationality of a subject of the King . . . That underlying element which binds every individual British subject to every other is the material on which the foundation of each government of our Empire is laid. Each subject of these Governments is one of his Majesty's subjects, and each Government is one of the Governments of the King." I have quoted this passage at length in order to show the French reader that English statesmen, and even the colleagues of the Foreign Secretary, who are so fond of contrasting English common sense with French logic, when it suits their purpose, can be as juridically-minded as any Continental jurist. It is idle to pick holes in Mr. Amery's fine-spun theory. One might, of course, point out that there is one government in the Empire which is not the government of the King but that of the "Emperor of India." Readers of M. André Maurois' *Disraeli* will not need to be reminded of the circumstances connected with the adoption of this title. But it is enough to say, that only a jurist, and a jurist of exceptional skill, can argue with plausibility that a King who is constitutionally bound, since the Imperial Conference of 1926, to give equal weight to the advice tendered him by the Prime Minister of Great Britain and the Prime Minister of Australia is not King in two different capacities in relation to the English and Australian peoples respectively. To regard loyalty to the one and indivisible Crown, as Mr. Amery does, as the "underlying element" in the government of the British Empire is to play with words. Divus Augustus and his successors might be made to play that part with some show of reality in the days of the Roman Empire. But to lay it down for a constitutional monarch in an era of democracy and republicanism is to mistake the shadow for the reality, or, to be more precise, to mistake the symbol for that which it symbolises.

For if the Monarchy survives and has even, as Lord Balfour has lately declared,[1] greatly increased its influence, it is not as a source of power but as a concrete symbol, such as all men, and Englishmen particularly, cherish, of common traditions and common purposes.

Two illustrations may suffice to make clear to French readers the hold which the Monarchy exercises over British minds.

On November 11, 1918, at 11 a.m., the present writer was looking out of a window at the Foreign Office, facing the Prime Minister's house in Downing Street. It was the moment of the Armistice. The church bells were ringing and in the narrow street a small crowd of some 50 or 100 persons began to collect. The Prime Minister, then popularly regarded as the organiser of victory, appeared at the window and I wondered whether I was not about to witness a historic demonstration. But nothing happened and after a short time the crowd, such as it was, began to drift away into the Park. They were making their way to join the thousands of their fellow-citizens who, in a spontaneous movement, had gone to Buckingham Palace to acclaim the King. Thus two days after the abdication of his German cousin, at a moment when thrones were toppling throughout Europe, the British monarch found himself the centre of an enthusiastic demonstration to celebrate the victory of the cause of democracy.

My other illustration concerns the ceremony when the remains of the Unknown Warrior were deposited in Westminster Abbey. The popular interest was intense and it

[1] In his preface to a new edition of Bagehot's *British Constitution*, Oxford, 1928.

was clear that the feelings of the nation were deeply stirred. I remarked to a friend who had attended the ceremony that for the first time there seemed a possibility of a republican movement in England, for the nation had responded in an unprecedented way to the call of an abstract idea, the symbol of a common sacrifice. "You are quite wrong," remarked my friend. "I listened to the talk of the crowd. They did not take that view of the ceremony at all. They were all asking themselves whether the unknown soldier might not be the one whom they themselves were mourning."

This need for a concrete embodiment of the British tradition explains the persistence of the Monarchy among a people who would be the first to cry out against the slightest extension of the royal power and in an Empire, several of whose governments, in deference to a democratic public opinion, have refused to recommend their citizens for titles of honour conferred by the King.

Thus the King as a symbol must not be confused with the Court as the apex of the social pyramid or with the Crown as an element in the Constitution. The social influence of the Court is no doubt important, but it is in no sense a binding element in the Empire. It wields more influence, for instance, in certain circles in the United States than in some British Dominions.

But if the King is a symbol, what does he symbolise? Wherein does the unity, of which he is the outward expression, consist? *What is the British Empire?*

The simplest answer to give to the fellow-countrymen of Renan is to refer them to his essay on the meaning of a nation. He defines nationality in spiritual values—common experience, common sacrifice, common achievement. It is only in spiritual values that the essence of the British

Empire can be defined. It is a habit of mind acquired
through common experience. But, unlike the narrower tie
of nationality, it is not a habit based on common culture,
on language or race or religion or any other such intimate
bond. It is a political tie, based on common experience in
the domain of public affairs. Perhaps the bond which unites
his Majesty's subjects is best expressed in four Latin
words—*idem sentire de republica*. Of these, the most important word is *sentire*. Not common opinions but a common outlook, a common way of regarding public affairs, a
common *public spirit* is the essence of the British experience and the British tradition.

It would, no doubt, be possible to push the analysis
farther, to indicate certain specific elements in the British
political outlook. We have already indicated above some
points in the English tradition, and it would be possible to
trace their influence both in the parts of the Empire colon-
ised from Great Britain and in the far more numerous
regions where British political institutions are in operation
among peoples with an entirely different inheritance. But
for this there is no space here. Suffice it to point out one
striking example which French observers can study for
themselves. Canada is now a member of the Council of the
League, and, as chance would have it, the representatives
whom she has hitherto sent to sit there have been men of
French stock. Those who have seen them at work can say
how far, and in what respects, they have assimilated British political habits and outlook. Or the same observation
may be made with regard to the Indian delegates who
attend the League of Nations Assembly.

This reflection leads on directly to the question of the
influence of the League of Nations upon the unity of the
Empire. Does the existence of the Geneva institution tend

to weaken the individuality of the Empire? To those who have observed it at close quarters the answer is clear. So far from weakening the Empire it is strengthening it. What is the *Société des Nations?* A society. And what is the value of a society? That it enables its members to manifest their special gifts and qualities in a *milieu* where they can be used to the best effect. It does not take a very profound knowledge of psychology to realise that the British members of the League of Nations feel more British in Geneva than they do in London. The psychological effect of an Imperial Conference, where British delegations from five continents are, for the most part, discussing matters on which their local interests are divided, is necessarily quite different from that of Geneva, where the British delegates are drawn naturally together in the face of foreign interests and, what is even more important, foreign habits of mind. "Do you not find these foreigners terribly trying?" remarked a British delegate to a friend on one occasion as he was passing out of a meeting in which the proceedings had not been conducted with British brevity and efficiency. "You forget," replied his interlocutor, long resident in England, whom the delegate had absent-mindedly taken for an Englishman, "you forget, Sir, that *you* are the foreigner here." Thus does Geneva provide a link of empire for Britons suffering beneath alien chairmanship in a strange country!

One might go farther and explain in detail the advantages which the League organization presents for the Empire by providing a convenient forum for the discussion of the many troublesome and controversial details which must arise between its scattered communities. In brief, it may be said that the League helps the Empire by *specialising* its problems of detail and thus aiding towards their solution on technical and non-controversial lines and by making its peoples more conscious of the larger problems on which they think and feel alike. This has certainly been the experience of the first eight years of the League and it seems likely to be continued. The League, in fact, represents for the Empire not a Euthanasia but a Koinonia.

We have reached the conclusion of our analysis. It remains to ask how far this amorphous multicellular political organism, this tentacular community with antennæ in every part of the globe, can be reconciled with traditional views of the State: and, if not, whether it or these views should be revised.

The answer, here as elsewhere, lies with the League of Nations.

In the world as it was in 1914 such a state as the British Empire is to-day would have been impossible. It could not have survived the strain and stress of contending national purposes. It can only survive to-day in a world organised for peace, in a world which is able to adapt its political institutions to a system of assured peace. Under such a system the policies of states will no longer be dominated by the fear of war and many questions which to-day are under the tight control of the central power will be handed over to technical bodies for handling along more scientific lines. But this relaxation of the powers of the state will only be possible when the peoples of the States comprising the League have convinced themselves that peace is indeed assured. The League is still far from exercising the authority which Englishmen, for instance, feel for their own law, or commanding the respect which drew Englishmen to their king's palace on Armistice Day. That it will acquire this authority and respect we are bound to believe: for, in a world where economic forces are becoming more

and more formidable, it is the only hope of the maintenance of the authority of *politics* in the ordering of men's
affairs, of the supremacy of *res publica* over *res privata*.
The growth of the League may indeed be slow; or it may
be far more rapid than seems likely from present-day tendencies. In any case, the worst criticism that can be made
against the present system of the British Empire—against
the third Empire, as it is called—is that it is adapted to a
world different from that of 1914, a world in which co-
operation has become the rule and in which the processes
of such co-operation have been perfected. For the successors of Edmund Burke and those who resisted the ideas of
the French Revolution, this may be a valid criticism: for
they lived exclusively by the lights of the past. But for
those for whom 1918 is another milestone on the road of
1789 it cannot fail to be of interest to note that the state
which is most closely associated with France in the solution of the problems of the post-war world has had the
faith to adopt a system which demands for its successful
operation the realisation of an idea—and of an idea to
which both peoples are pledged by a common signature.

## IX

## INTERNATIONAL ORGANIZATION
## ITS PROSPECTS AND LIMITATIONS[1]

### I

THERE are numerous indications that American public opinion is once more devoting serious attention to the problem of the better organization of international relations. But if the discussion is to lead to the practical results which are hoped from it, if it is to rise above the atmosphere of thoughtless idealistic phrase-making and equally thoughtless cynicism that together contributed to the deadlock in which the problem has too long been involved, it must be based upon a clear analysis of the existing condition in the various fields of international organization, of the difficulties with which schemes of closer union are confronted, and of the directions in which advance can most usefully be attempted. It is the object of the following pages, if but in the briefest outline, to attempt such a survey.

The simplest and clearest way of approaching the subject is to begin by setting forth the nature of the material with which international relations are concerned. When we have before us a view of the business which has to be conducted, we shall be better able to form a judgment on the machinery needed for its effective discharge. No business man would dream of organizing an office before he had a knowledge of the business that passed through it. Yet a good deal of the current comment on the problem of international relations is carried on in complete detachment

[1]Contributed to the *Atlantic Monthly*, September, 1923.

(to use no stronger word) from the nature of the material with which it is professedly concerned. A survey of this material will enable us at the same time to measure the change in the character of international contacts which has taken place during the last two generations, and to appreciate the change in international machinery which has already taken place as its natural consequence. The school of writers in Europe and elsewhere who maintain that the fabric of civilization is dissolving and that the world is relapsing into chaos are simply ignorant of the facts.

The business of international relations, the business that is arising out of the relations between sovereign states, transacted through public officials, may to-day be grouped roughly under five heads.

First, to begin with the easiest, there are routine matters arising out of international contacts. These fill the greater number of the files which occupy the desks of the officials concerned with international relations in foreign offices and elsewhere. Two groups of business may be specified among them. There is the material arising out of the appointment and transference, the regular reports and special recommendations, of ambassadors, ministers, consuls, and other officials residing abroad; and there is the material arising out of the network of treaties concluded on what may be called the non-contentious side of international relations—the prevention of disease and crime, the improvement of communications, the promotion of science and scientific standards in the numerous regions in which mankind is moving, by general agreement, toward a greater uniformity. All this is part of what has increasingly become in recent generations the fabric of a common civilization.

The second group of material, which is distinguished by no clear line of demarcation from the first, deals with what may be described as routine matters outside the zone of agreed principles. We pass here insensibly from routine administration to diplomacy proper. All civilized states are agreed as to the desirability of extraditing criminals, of facilitating postal, telegraphic, wireless, and other means of communication, of providing effective quarantine regulations against plague, promoting safety at sea, and so on. But when we pass to business, however insignificant, involving such issues as the Open Door, the equality of races, the control of immigration in the home-land or in dependencies, the Monroe Doctrine, we pass from a region of agreed principles to a region of difficulty, contention, and possible danger. Such business cannot be transacted by standing upon agreed first principles and working out convenient ways of putting them into practice. It must be transacted by avoiding the discussion of first principles, or, at any rate, their logical and methodical application, and working out a provisional arrangement such as will meet the immediate need of the moment without arousing popular passion or prejudice. This is the characteristic work of foreign offices and ambassadors. It is this which distinguishes their work, and the qualities required from it, from the work of administration in the domestic departments of government and from the work of administrators, at Geneva or elsewhere, who are carrying out the provisions of a general treaty.

The third class of business, which impinges closely on the second, is what is described, sometimes with bated breath, as "high policy." It is concerned with the handling of issues arising not out of ordinary routine contacts, whether in the non-contentious or the contentious zone, but out of the *policies* of the powers, and especially of the Great Powers. The difference between a principle and a policy, in foreign affairs as elsewhere, is the difference between passivity and self-assertion. Disagreement about principles may leave the waters of diplomacy unruffled; but it is of the essence of policy to awaken life and movement. There is nothing regrettable about this. It is as right and healthy for a state to have a foreign policy as for an individual to manifest his personality. A state without a foreign policy is a dead state. If, for fear of the resulting contacts and clashes, civilized states and their foreign ministers forbore to put forward policies, and thus abstained from seeking to incorporate in the general world-order principles which they held to be of value, mankind would be spared the risk of warfare only to perish of inanition.

If Britain stands for the lowering of fiscal barriers and a one-power standard of naval strength as essential to her life and security; if Japan stands for the recognition of the equality of nations as essential to her self-respect; if Australia stands for the exclusion of non-white immigrants as essential to the survival of her national personality; if the United States stands for the Monroe Doctrine, and the Open Door in the Far East and elsewhere, nothing is to be gained by attempting to repress, conceal, or ignore these fixed and firm expressions of national will and determination. They are indeed far more dangerous repressed than expressed.

On the other hand, everything depends on the manner of their expression. Generally speaking, it is not nowadays in policies themselves that danger lies, but in their handling. There have been criminal autocracies, as recently as 1914; but the criminal democracy is not a real source of peril. It is the unwise, ignorant, and precipitate democracy, pushing a policy, not in itself unreasonable, by unreasonable and unimaginative means, which constitutes the danger-point at the present time. And it is the main function and justification of foreign secretaries and diplomats to promote the fixed policies and permanent interests of their countries in a manner so persuasive and reasonable as to make them intelligible to peoples who necessarily view the same issues from very different angles of vision.

Wise statesmanship can go far in the promotion even of contentious and difficult policies without evolving active displeasure or bringing about a crisis. But it remains true, even under the most prudent and tactful régime, that complications with a foreign power will occur sometimes, as in the Venezuela boundary dispute of 1895, from unforeseen and relatively trivial causes. Such complications involve the fourth class of international business, the material which, whatever its nature, or the importance or insignificance of the opposing state, may be described as *disputes*. It is in the technique of the handling of this class of material, as we shall see, that very notable improvements in international organization have been made in recent years.

Finally, affecting and affected by the work of those who conduct foreign relations, but not actually administered by them are the armed forces upon which states rely, in the last resort, for the maintenance of their independence and the promotion of their policies. The acutest form of international contact is war.

## II

Having thus rapidly surveyed the material of international relations, we may turn to consider the organization available for dealing with it.

The recognized method of transacting international business is through a special department of state, the Foreign Office or Ministry of External Affairs, with its staff of ambassadors, ministers, and consuls abroad, in regular communication with it. The Foreign Office as an institution dates back to the middle of the seventeenth century, and the institution of permanent legations, adopted by Britain, France, Spain, and Germany as early as the end of the fifteenth century, became regular among the civilized states in the seventeenth century. Foreign Offices and their agents abroad were, in fact, until comparatively recently, apart from the personal activities of monarchs and heads of states, practically the sole channel of international intercourse. Not only the routine business in normal times, but the conferences and congresses which supervened in time of crisis were left in the hands of Foreign Secretaries and their personnel. The "staff of secretaries and Foreign Office assistants" with which Lord Salisbury and his chief repaired to the Berlin Congress in 1878 did not differ in composition from the staff which accompanied Castlereagh to Vienna in 1814.

But in the period between the Berlin Congress of 1878 and the Paris Conference of 1918 an important, if little noticed, change occurred in the conduct of international relations. A number of routine matters belonging to the first, or non-contentious, class specified above were withdrawn from the management and, in some cases, from the control of Foreign Offices, and handed over to special bodies created by treaty for that purpose. The process, in fact, had begun a few years before 1878 and was a direct and inevitable result of the nineteenth-century inventions and the immense increase in international contacts which resulted from them. The most important of these new

agencies may be briefly enumerated. The International
Telegraph Office of the International Telegraph Union was
established in 1868. The International Post Office of the
Universal Postal Union was established in Berne in 1874.
The International Office of Weights and Measures for
states using the metric system was established in Paris in
1875. The International Union for the Publication of
Customs Tariffs, with its office in Brussels, dates from
1890; the Central Office of International Transports at
Berne also from 1890; the International Institute of Agriculture at Rome from 1905, and the International Health
Office in Paris from 1907.

Two reflections suggest themselves from a perusal of
this list. In the first place, the subjects which it covers are
not only non-contentious but of a kind to invite uniformity—in other words, management by an international
authority. Posts and telegraphs, weights and measures,
transport, the prevention of disease, and the dissemination
of information about tariffs and crops, are all matters
which can safely be withdrawn from the day-by-day
management and vigilance of separate sovereign governments and allowed to become what may be described as
international material. I remember once calling on a
clergyman of my acquaintance just after he had returned
from a visit to the hospital. I asked him whether he confined his ministrations to patients of his own denomina-
tion. "Did you ever hear," he replied, "of Jewish dropsy,
Presbyterian measles, or Roman Catholic housemaid's
knee?" The material of the International Health Office is
material from which every drop of the bitter waters of
nationalism has been squeezed out. It is, therefore, material which can be studied impersonally, supernationally,
scientifically, in the interests and under the auspices of

mankind as a whole. And what is true of health is true, if in a lesser degree, of most of the other material for which international unions and offices had been created before the war.

The other reflection which leaps to the mind from the list is that the matters with which it is concerned have now ceased to be Foreign Office material, even at the domestic end. Posts and telegraphs have passed from the Foreign Secretary to the Postmaster-general; tariffs, weights and measures, and transport to the Department of Commerce or Board of Trade; crop reports to the Department or Board of Agriculture, and health to the Ministry of Health. In other words, contact is in these cases no longer between Foreign Office and Foreign Office, or between Foreign Office and this or that international board, but between the specialized departments of the various governments and the international boards concerned with the same material. Instead of a single form of contact, through the agency traditionally and rightly concerned with the maintenance of the national interest and prestige, we now have a whole series of contacts through agencies established to promote human welfare in various departments of social activity. States which used to touch one another with a single finger, the finger of power, now meet with a handclasp in a spirit of collaboration and joint human service.

So far we have been dealing with international relations prior to the World War. But in this, as in other spheres of international organization, the war, by creating new problems, forced men to take stock of the progress already achieved. For the contacts between the Allied states in the war were not exclusively military, naval, and diplomatic, as in previous wars, but extended along the whole line of governmental activity. There was hardly a department which was not required to contribute from its expert service to the Allied collaboration. By the autumn of 1918 the Interallied organization had reached a point of development far beyond the wildest dreams of pre-war administrative internationalism. Never before in human history has the world been so regimented in its activities, from Iceland to Australia and from tonnage to tobacco, as in the closing months of the war. This amazing achievement of collaboration disappeared with the disappearance of the common purpose which had sustained it; but its administrative experience remains. The lessons to be drawn from the experiment have been ably and lucidly summarized by Sir Arthur Salter, one of the men most closely concerned in it, in his volume on the *Allied Shipping Control;* and from his pages we can learn of the prospects and pitfalls of international organization in the field of noncontentious activities. What is wanted, he sums up, to make international administration more effective is "morally, a great effort of faith," and "administratively, a great effort of decentralization."

Future historians, looking back over the process of world-integration, are likely to fix on Article XXIV of the Covenant of the League of Nations as the most epoch-making section of that much-discussed document. That article, which has lain quietly under the hedge while the battle raged to and fro over its more obtrusive colleagues, lays it down that "There shall be placed under the direction of the League all international bureaux already established by general treaties if the parties to such treaties consent"; and adds that "all such international bureaux and all commissions for the regulation of matters of international interest hereafter constituted shall be placed under the direction of the League."

It is by virtue of this article that the Secretariat at Geneva does a large and expanding part of its day-by-day work. The work of the Secretariat is not, as is commonly supposed, a work of "centralization." It is a work of co-ordination. Its significance lies, not in the importance of the material that it is handling, or in the number and authority of the governments which allow part of their domestic concerns to pass through its hands, but in the fact that it is engaged in working out a satisfactory technique for the collaboration of governments in the handling of problems which are at once too intricate and domestic to be centralized and too international in their ramifications to be solved by individual governments acting in isolation. We are a long way yet from the full possibilities of administrative internationalism. There are a host of thorny problems—the conservation of the world's mineral resources is an outstanding example—which are not yet ripe for the sober Geneva technique. But the mould is there ready to hand; and when the public opinion of the world is prepared for the experiment, the metal can be poured into it.

So far we have been concerned entirely with the first, or non-contentious, class of international contacts. It was necessary to emphasize the transformation that has taken place in the transaction of this class of business, because it indicates the general drift and direction of international organization. The world cannot be integrated by sentimental crusades against war or by ingenious devices to conceal divergencies of high policy. Diplomacy is, at best, only a makeshift, and propaganda, however well-meaning, is hardly even a makeshift. Integration must begin with the material that is ready for it. Fifty years ago the world was not ready, Britain was not ready, for an opium policy.

What is being done for opium and dangerous drugs to-day may be practicable for oil, or nickel, or tin to-morrow.

What is important, let it be repeated, is not what has already been achieved, but the testing of the soundness of the method of procedure. We know now that it is possible, when public opinion is ripe for it, to take a problem "out of politics," or, to be more accurate, out of diplomacy, and to entrust it to a body of men drawn from many nations who have the training and outlook, not of the negotiator and old-time statesman, but of the doctor and the scientist. This is what is meant when it is claimed that Geneva has given the world for the first time an international civil service, an organized body of servants of mankind. This surely marks one of the greatest advances ever made in the art of managing human affairs. Yet it has been effected without doing violence to existing principles and ideals. It does not reject democracy and substitute the tyranny of the expert, nor does it invalidate national sovereignty by the imposition of a centralized oligarchy. It merely enables the free self-governing peoples of the world, if and so long as they desire it, to employ the best men and the best means for collaboration in problems which no government, however powerful, can solve for itself alone.

### III

We pass now to our second class of business, the zone of contention, difficulty, and danger. What means exist for improving the handling of this still essentially diplomatic material? It has already been said that governments, in dealing with this material, are compelled to avoid the discussion of principles. There are few more fatal errors in statesmanship than the attempt to push a principle, however apparently unexceptionable, which important parties to the negotiation are not prepared to accept. In the existing state of opinion in Australia about the equality of races, to take an instance replete with possibilities of controversy, it is idle to seek to lay down a general principle as the basis of an agreed world-policy. It may be that in a few generations' time Australians will feel as much ashamed of their present attitude toward non-white races as Englishmen do of their mid-nineteenth-century opium-policy. It is, however, much more likely that the problem conveniently summed up in the slogan, racial equality, will be seen in a different light; that numerous interrelations, at present unperceived, will be brought into view; and that, if the problem as we see it now has not been solved, some elements of it will have been disengaged and found susceptible of non-contentious treatment. A survey of these and kindred attitudes suggests that the existence of strong feeling among any people or peoples in opposition to what seems to be an enlightened and progressive world-policy should be taken as an indication that the question has not been sufficiently explored.

What then is the line of advance? Surely it should be an advance in double column. The diplomatist, working necessarily by rule of thumb, meeting each crisis and difficulty as it arises, must keep in close touch with the prevailing sentiment of the opposing parties. Meanwhile, outside the range of day-by-day solutions and provisional formulæ, students of politics must be attacking the problem from every angle, seeking to probe its difficulties and to disengage some elements which admit of a more scientific treatment. The fact that a problem is not yet ripe for scholars and scientists to manage is no reason why they should abstain from considering it. On the contrary, it is a challenge to submit it to the process, first of research and then of expert conference, in the hope that conference may lead in due time to consultation by governments, and that the recommendations thus arrived at may eventually form the basis of an agreed policy.

Scholarship and statesmanship necessarily dwell in different worlds, as Plato told us long ago; but in this at least Geneva has brought his *Republic* to life, that it has provided, and will increasingly provide, for their meeting and collaboration. Diplomacy is still necessarily diplomacy, and rash attempts to impose solutions by pressure and propaganda may have broken down; but the philosophers and the engineers, the economists, the chemists and the geologists, the doctors and the lawyers, have been enticed down from their ivory tower to the consulting-room, to their own advantage and that of mankind.

In one of these departments, indeed, that of law, a definite and fundamental relationship has been established with international politics. The International Court of Justice has, at present, but a restricted scope of activity. Its work is confined to questions which arise under treaties, or within the very limited area of agreed principles known as "established international law." But we have only to look back, not to Grotius, but to Austin, to realize what an achievement it is to have secured any real *terra firma* at all amid the hazards and vicissitudes of the world's affairs; and the setting-up of the Hague Court, like the institution of the Geneva Secretariat, marks, in Mr. Hoover's words, a "sound and sure step" toward the ultimate establishment of world-wide "processes of justice and moral right."

In the third sphere, that of high policy, there has been, as a result of the war, a remarkable advance in the understanding of the possibilities and limitations of organization.

The first result of the war was to drive men to simple and ultra-idealistic solutions. The war, it was argued, had arisen out of the diplomatic struggle between the Triple Alliance and the Triple Entente, itself a product of the European tradition of the Balance of Power. The post-war settlement therefore should provide for the disappearance of all alliances and for the extinction of the idea of a balancing equipoise. They should be replaced by a comprehensive partnership of peoples working with single-minded community of purpose in a League of Nations. In other words, it was proposed to replace Triple-Alliance policy, Triple-Entente policy, and American Monroe-Doctrine policy by world-policy, carried on by the powers, especially the Great Powers, in close and organized co-operation.

In the light of what has happened in the last four and a half years this notion may well seem fantastic to-day, and there are some who will even deny that it was ever entertained in the framing of the Covenant. But it must be remembered that in 1918 men were living under the impression of the close war-time collaboration of the Allies, and that, on the British side at any rate, there had been an encouraging precedent. When the framers of the "Cecil draft" devised their plan of the Council of the League, or Conference, as they preferred to call it, they modeled it deliberately on the Conference of Premiers in the British Commonwealth, one of whose main functions was, and is, to arrive at a common foreign policy for six or more peoples in five continents. It is true that, as General Smuts has remarked, a common policy for the British Empire must necessarily be drawn up on very simple lines; but the difficulties which have since arisen, in connection with the Japanese Alliance, the Near East, and other questions, were not then foreseen; and even now, in spite of all, and with necessary modifications, the Conference of Premiers to frame a common British foreign policy remains a standing institution.

But what is barely practicable for Britain has proved totally impracticable for the world at large. It is true that the experiment was never given a fair chance; for when room on the Council was found for four (now six) so-called representatives of the lesser states, appropriately called "states with special interests," any chance that it would be used by the Great Powers as an organ of high policy was dissipated. But it is probable that, in any case, the idea of such a world-organ was too ambitious. The questions that form the material of high policy are too various and scattered, the passions and interests involved are too diverse, the responsibilities too unequally divided between continent and continent, and, above all, the angles of vision from which they are approached are too divergent, to permit of the framing of a real partnership. Quite apart from the breakdown of this side of the League's original design, all sorts of natural causes, psychological, political, and economic, have been operating since the Armistice to drive peoples and governments away from the idea of world-partnership in high policy back to the idea of special affinities and alliances.

We need only mention the close association between France and Belgium, the Little Entente between Czechoslovakia, Yugoslavia, and Rumania, with which Poland is in such close touch, the revival of Monroe Doctrine sentiment in the United States, and the Four-Power pact limited to the regions of the Pacific.

But these new groupings, closely examined, bear a very different character from that of the traditional European system, and give a clear indication of the direction in which we must look for a reconciliation between the vigorous pursuit of national interests and the necessities of a harmonious world-order. In the first place they are public, not secret; in the second place they are regional and not general; thirdly, and most important of all, they are not merely compatible with, but actually sanctioned by, the Covenant of the League and therefore included within its larger framework. As for non-contentious issues Article XXIII is all-important, so Article XXI is pivotal for the future conduct of high policy.

"Nothing in this Covenant," it runs, "shall be deemed to affect the validity of international engagements such as treaties of arbitration and regional understandings like the Monroe Doctrine for securing the maintenance of peace."

Thus the present possibilities for international organization in the field of high policy seem clearly indicated. There is no super-government. We are far even from true international co-operation. We are limited to regional co-operation, backed up, on the one hand, by an elastic concert of the Great Powers, operating through conferences, as and when the need arises, and, on the other, by formal and strongly guaranteed precautions against a breach of the world's peace. The post-war world still finds France more interested in her eastern frontier than in the Far East, the United States more interested in Panama and China than in the Rhine, Australia more interested in the Pacific islands than in Upper Silesia, Czechoslovakia and Poland more interested in the evolution of Russia than in the Tacna-Arica controversy.

Those who are disappointed with this situation, and with a world in which (to quote from a disillusioned member of the Geneva Assembly) "nations are only internationally minded where their own interests are not immediately concerned," should remember that the substitution of democracy for autocracy in the conduct of the policy of the Great Powers has necessarily tended, in the early stages, to the advantage of passion as against reason. It was easier for Bismarck and Lord Salisbury in the eighteen-eighties to take long-distance views on questions of national interest than it was for Mr. Lloyd George and M. Clémenceau in 1919. On the other hand the reader of Bismarck's dispatches and of Lord Salisbury's life rises with a vivid sense of the definite advance brought about in the conduct of high policy since their time.

The framework of the League may seem a weak and flimsy bulwark against the forces of national growth and self-assertion which it is designed to check or channel. But as public opinion comes to realize the meaning and incidence of its various safeguards; as, when occasion arises, its provisions against the validity of secret engagements, against sudden resort to war, against inequitable commercial policies and proved abuses in colonial government, are brought into play; it will become increasingly clear, that, if the ship of high policy is still tossing on a rough and partly uncharted ocean, at least she has a compass and strong anchors, and a crew pledged and eager to bring her to port.

We have already encroached upon the fourth region—that of disputes. Here Articles XII to XVII of the League, together with the Bryan treaties, mark an advance which has not yet been fully realized. They commit civilized states to the doctrine that to resort to war without inquiry and delay, in however good a cause, is an international crime.

In other words, they make, once and for all, a broad distinction too often ignored in discussing the events of 1914, between the predisposing and determining causes of a breach of the peace. This distinction is a direct result of the interdependence of the modern world. Historians of the nineteenth and previous centuries have not been wont to ask who lit the match which embroiled Piedmont with Austria or the Kingdom of Naples, or William III with Louis XIV, or Queen Elizabeth with Philip II. Bismarck, who manœuvred declarations of war against his master both in 1866 and in 1870, was perhaps the first to see the importance of formal correctitude in the initiation of hostilities. But it was the Austrian ultimatum to Serbia, followed by the German ultimata to Russia, France, and Belgium, which brought home to public opinion that, in our modern large-scale world, the way in which a dispute is handled is of more concern to mankind than its actual merits. All that remains, after the formulation of the League's provisions against a breach of the peace, is to ensure that their sanctions will be effective. This is the object of the joint scheme of disarmament and guarantees, partly general and partly regional in scope, which Lord Robert Cecil and the Temporary Mixed Commission on Disarmament are preparing for the consideration of the League Assembly next September. Its details are too complicated to be discussed here, and the degree to which military force, sea power, and economic power are to co-operate in the enforcement of peace will form the subject of much debate; but the general principle, that of the organized co-operation of the police forces of civilization against a law-breaking state, or, in other words, the organization of Might behind Right, may surely be regarded as acceptable to practically every school of opinion.

Our argument has already carried us forward from disputes to armaments. Of armaments in general there is indeed little to be said. They are a symptom, not a disease; a thermometer by which to register the fever in the blood of the world's body politic, not a germ to be extirpated by direct action. The road to the reduction of armaments lies through the promotion of confidence by wise policy. And the road to the promotion of confidence in statesmanship is the same as in any other department of responsible trusteeship—through a large-minded prudence in the assumption of obligations, a strict and even pedantic loyalty in their observance, through continuity in the framing of policies, tact and consistency and patience in their promotion, and a keen and delicate sense of what is owing both to the comity of nations and to the interests of which statesmanship is the trustee. And to statesmanship of this order in the post-war world, at last provided with sure precautions and anchorage against a drift to disaster, to men such as Cecil, Bourgeois, and Beneš, in the Old World, and to others whom it would be invidious to mention in the New, surely we may apply the words which Newman used of the scholar in his ideal university—

"The intellect which has been disciplined to the perfection of its powers, which knows and thinks while it knows, which has learned to leaven the dense mass of facts and events with the elastic force of reason, such an intellect cannot be partial, cannot be exclusive, cannot be at a loss, cannot but be patient, collected, and majestically calm, because it discerns the end in every beginning, the origin in every end, and law in every interruption, the limit in each delay; because it ever knows where it stands and how its path lies from one point to another."

# X

## THE PROSPECTS OF DEMOCRACY[1]

I HAVE entitled my subject "the Prospects of Democracy"; but my object is not to prophesy the future, but simply to analyse existing conditions and perhaps also to open out a fresh field of study for the Institute.

My thesis is a simple one and can be stated in a sentence: *We live in an age of democracy, but democracy has not yet discovered its appropriate institutions.*

President Wilson, in a famous phrase, spoke of the War as an effort to "make the world safe for democracy." That result has been achieved. The world has been made safe for democracy. But democracy has not yet been made safe for mankind.

We of this generation are conscious that we are passing through a time of crisis and readjustment. But it is not, as is often said, a crisis of democracy: the survival of democracy is not in doubt. It is a crisis of constitutionalism, a crisis in the conduct of public affairs and in the very art of government. That is what makes the problem so appropriate for study and discussion in this Institute.

What, you will ask, do I mean by democracy?

Democracy is a form of society—a form of society which has not yet found its form of government. We speak of democracy as a form of government; but, in point of fact, as we shall see, democracy has hitherto been carrying on its public duties with political institutions taken over from the preceding régime and not yet adapted to its own conditions.

[1] Substance of an address delivered at the Royal Institute of International Affairs on November 8, 1927, Viscount Haldane in the chair.

I will not attempt an analysis of what constitutes a democratic society. To us Europeans, who necessarily see it in contrast with the conditions which it has superseded, its chief characteristic appears to be negative—the absence of inherited privilege. But it is better, at this stage of our experience, to fix our notion of it from concrete examples rather than to attempt a detailed analysis. The United States and Switzerland were democracies in 1914; Austria-Hungary and Russia were not, but the territories comprised in them, with the single exception of Hungary—where the *ancien régime* still lingers on in moribund form—have become democracies, as a result of the War and the social revolution that followed it.

The United States is sometimes described, by a certain class of critics, as a plutocracy, by which is meant that the effective political power is in the hands, not of the elected representatives of the people, but of an oligarchy of wealth. But even if the most extreme allegations on this subject were proved true, twentieth-century American society would still remain undeniably democratic. Nobody who is familiar with both sides of the Atlantic could doubt the use of the term.

Perhaps the simplest way of bringing out the meaning of democracy is to point to some characteristic figures. Metternich and Bismarck, who spent their lives in stubborn resistance against the ideas of the French Revolution, are typical of the old social order: so, on the opposite side of the Atlantic, was George Washington. Contrast them, not only with great constitutional leaders such as a Lincoln, a Masaryk, or a Branting, but with the less familiar type of popular leadership embodied in a Mussolini, a Lenin or a Pilsudski. These so-called dictators are worlds away from the absolute or semi-absolute rulers of pre-War

Europe from a Francis Joseph or a Nicholas II. They are members of the rank and file of mankind who have reached power by their own personality. Lenin, it is true, was an aristocrat, carried to supremacy over the ruins of an aristocracy; but he was a belated and lonely example of his class. His case is but one of those occasional exceptions which serve to emphasise the rule. For the world in which the modern "dictator," whatever his origin, has to exercise and defend his power is the world of large-scale trade and industry, of railways and telephones, of the cinema and the radio, of compulsory education and the popular Press—in fact, of what we are accustomed to call modern civilization.

One of the special features of that civilization, arising precisely out of its large-scale character, is its levelling tendency. With men in masses to be provided for, it finds it easier to avoid fine distinctions. Thus it puts quantity before quality, and whilst it undoubtedly levels up from below, it also levels down from above. It is predisposed to mediocrity. This is a point to which we shall return.

Another reproach often made against democracy by defenders of the old order is that it tends towards instability. To this it may be answered that it has never yet, in Europe at any rate, had a fair trial. The nineteenth century was a transition period during which democracy, viewed as an international force, was a movement of protest and often of revolt. The War, by sweeping away the last vestiges of the mediæval system, of the Holy Roman Empire in Central Europe, of the Byzantine Empire in Russia and of the Islamic Middle Ages, turned democracy from a minority into a majority force, from an Opposition into a Government.

Thus to-day democracy, socially triumphant, is faced

for the first time, on the international plane, with the problem of government. Can it maintain political power? Can it develop appropriate political institutions? Can it, in other words, achieve stability? The question is as old as Thucydides. It still waits for an answer.

But, if the event is doubtful, one thing is clear. The issue to-day is no longer between democracy and the old order. The *ancien régime*, with its Bourbons and its Hapsburgs, its Hohenzollerns and its Romanoffs, has passed away beyond recall. Even if its ghosts returned to sit on their thrones, they would not reign. Democracy to-day has a new Opposition to face. Its arch-enemy is not inherited privilege, but private power. It is government itself which is in danger. The cause of democracy is bound up with the cause of public power, of "res publica," as opposed to "res privata."

Let us now consider the problem before us from another point of view, from the angle of government.

Government is the system by which the public affairs of a community are carried on. The character of a government must therefore be closely related to the character of the affairs with which it is concerned. What a government is depends on what a government has to do. In other words, political institutions must serve social needs and must correspond to social conditions. Once this is grasped, it is not difficult to diagnose the *malaise* from which we are suffering.

The social conditions of the civilized world have been completely transformed within the last hundred and fifty years, whilst its political institutions, based on tradition, are still largely unchanged in form. This disharmony between social conditions and political institutions has far-reaching consequences. Certain influences resulting from it may be noted at once.

The traditional character of our political institutions has accustomed us to acquiesce in a difference between appearance and reality in the sphere of politics. We are used to the notion that governments are never what they seem. This has led to much insincerity and even hypocrisy and to not a little confusion of thought.

One consequence of this has been to place a grave hindrance in the way of the study of government. Much of what is known in academic circles as "political science" is a mere playing with words. The thinker in his study and the professor in his lecture-room are too often using ideas and categories which bear no relation to the real object of their study. This is particularly marked in the case of Continental writers, who are more legalistically inclined than ourselves and more easily attracted by abstract and symmetrical schemes. Thus quite recently I have come across writings by professors of standing dealing with the British Commonwealth and the League of Nations which are misleading from the first page to the last. Such writers start from the traditional distinctions of political science— Monarchy and Republic, *Bundesstaat* and *Staatenbund* and the rest—and try to fit reality into this bed of Procrustes. To those visiting America for the first time the advice has been given to forget all that they have ever heard of it and to see it with fresh eyes. To those who enter public life after a study of the traditional political science the advice is equally appropriate.

But there is an even graver consequence flowing from this disharmony. It has brought about a dangerous differentiation between political and economic institutions— between the institutions of what used to be considered government proper and the institutions of the system through which we are fed and clothed. Whilst our political institutions have remained rooted in ancient habit, in the economic sphere we have developed a great and wide-spread new system corresponding with some approxima-tion to our modern economic needs. But this new system is private, not public: it is outside the constitution. The result is that not only are our private needs—if we can call them so—better provided for than our public needs, but also that private power, with its new and up-to-date type of organization, has an immense advantage over public power. In the sphere of government we are, in fact, attempting to do twentieth-century work with eighteenth-century instruments.

Let us now look a little more closely at the conditions with which government is faced. The process which we call the Industrial Revolution has brought about a greater change in the lives and habits of mankind in five or six generations than occurred, not in hundreds but in thousands of years preceding it. Alexander and Julius Cæsar come to life again in 1777 would have been less astonished than the men of 1777 would be to-day. The change has been brought about by the practical applica-tions of natural science. The old small-scale, hand-run world which, now that it has passed away, we fondly imagine suited us so well, has gone and in its place there is an international economic system which has created a world-wide interdependence.

Technically and officially, the world is still divided into sections called States; but for the purposes of its very efficient economic system, through which we live, it is a single unit.

Now in the nineteenth century, while this great change was proceeding, this clean division between the political and the economic, between the world of States and the world of business, was generally accepted and proved not altogether unworkable in practice. It may be compared to the division of the physical globe into land and water. The classical economists and their pupils of the Manchester School thought of the world as fluid. They conceived of the movement of business as pervading the earth and passing unimpeded across oceans and frontiers. Conditions, no doubt, had not yet become entirely liquid; but they were fast becoming so, and they felt justified in making the free flow of men and goods one of the assumptions of their thinking. It is true that both Adam Smith and Ricardo in isolated passages betray an uneasy sense that political or even deeper social considerations may interfere with the pure workings of economic science. Every now and then, so to speak, the smooth progress of their economic vessel encounters a political reef. But they did no more than mark it incidentally on their chart, and continue their voyage.[1] Political economy, in spite of its name, remained non-political. Meanwhile, government remained solidly attached to *terra firma*, concerned almost exclusively with problems of justice, defence, education and other matters remote from the economic sphere. Up to the end of the third quarter of the nineteenth century the general movement in Europe, even in the non-democratic States, was towards the curtailment of the powers of government. The influence of the French Revolution and of the Reform movement in England in sweeping away abuses and curtailing privileges worked to this end. There were indeed points, such as the tariff,

[1] For some quotations in illustration of this see Appendix I.

where government and business came into contact; but
on the whole the two moved in separate orbits with little
mutual interrelation. This was true, broadly speaking,
both of Europe and of the United States.

This nineteenth-century tendency to keep the political
and economic life of mankind in separate compartments
was greatly strengthened by the Socialist movement. It
will surely be recognized as one of the ironies of history
that nineteenth-century Socialism, by its attempt to
make use of the national State as the instrument of its
economic policy, delayed and so finally prevented the
consolidation of economic power in national political units.
The revolutionary doctrines of Socialism were equally un-
palatable to the governments and the business men of
the day; and their dislike of the ends blinded them as to
the interesting possibilities of the means. State association
in commerce and industry became mixed up in men's
minds with the class struggle, the dictatorship of the pro-
letariat and other disagreeable watchwords, and thus the
opportunity of fortifying the national State by supple-
menting its political power by economic power was allowed
to slip by. As things were it was only in Germany, and
only in the decade before 1914, in the activities of men like
Helfferich, that a systematic attempt was made to use
economic power for political purposes. This negative
service by an international movement, compelled, contrary
to its own principles, to preach and organize on a national
basis, may come, paradoxically enough, to rank as the
greatest contribution of nineteenth-century Socialism to
political development.

The War opened men's eyes. It became clear to us all
that the political and the economic, government and
business, cannot be kept in separate compartments, if

only because every modern State has to take account of economic organization in considering its system of national defence. Four years of war and blockade and counter-blockade brought it home, not only to the belligerents but sometimes quite as insistently to the neutrals, that, in the world as it now is, economic problems form a part, and perhaps the most important part, of governmental policy. It is, in fact, no more possible to disentangle political issues from economic than it is to maintain the time-honoured distinction between "domestic" and "foreign" affairs. Before the War even as close and as perennially youthful an observer as Lord Bryce, in planning out the material for his book on democracy, could still relegate "Democracy and Foreign Policy" to a separate chapter. The War and its sequel have taught us that there is hardly a domestic problem which can be mentioned—take only the example of the "sheltered trades"—which does not need to be considered also in relation to extra-domestic forces. No student of public affairs or practical administrator can to-day mark off a group of problems and label them as material of foreign policy. In a word, the effect of the Industrial Revolution, and of the War, which first opened our eyes as to its full significance in the political sphere, has been to make the material of politics as fully international as the material of economics has been recognized to be from the time of the classical economists onward. States are no longer to-day self-contained sections of the earth's surface with a few outlying interests which are called "foreign affairs." An international outlook and a wide knowledge of the world are as greatly and as continuously needed in every branch of high political administration as in the head office of a bank or any other business.

But while the material of government has thus become enlarged, so as to embrace the whole world, there has been a parallel movement going on during the last five or six generations which has had the contrary effect on the mind of those responsible for public affairs. If the Industrial Revolution has given us large-scale economic problems, the democratic movement proceeding from the French Revolution has given us small-scale political minds. Simultaneously with the growth of this vast new system of world-wide interdependence, political power in Europe, North America and Australia, and increasingly in other continents, has been placed in the hands of the great mass of the people. This has greatly intensified the disharmony between political and economic institutions.

The natural effect of democracy upon public affairs is to intensify public opinion, especially on questions which appeal immediately to the ordinary man. An active public opinion tends to promote group thinking concentrated on local interests. The extension of political power, or of the sense of a right to such power, has brought into existence the movement, in essence psychological rather than political, for what has been described as "self-determination." What this has, in fact, denoted is the emergence of an increasing number of local units of public opinion, claiming the right to affirm, and even on occasion to enforce, their own particular feeling or interest.

One symptom of this has been the spread of the idea of the "nation-State," which has acted as a fissiparous influence breaking up large political units into constituent elements based on local centres of opinion. The nation-State in itself is, as Lord Acton pointed out some seventy years ago and President Masaryk has never ceased to emphasize, an inherent absurdity. It does not correspond to the pre-War, the present or any possible future political grouping of the world. But the movement ran its course in nineteenth-century Europe and is spreading its influence in Asia and elsewhere, because it provides a convenient channel for local opinion and local sentiment. As a result, not only are there more States in Europe than there were before the War, but the smaller States, both old and newly established, count for considerably more than they did. Pre-War diplomacy paid attention, broadly speaking, only to the Great Powers. On the chessboard to which Metternich and Bismarck devoted so much skill and ingenuity the large pieces held almost undisputed sway. But on the new post-War chessboard, at Geneva and elsewhere, there are a number of pawns and most of them are very much alive.

Nor is the movement of self-determination confined to political groups. It extends to innumerable other forms of common interest and sentiment. New organizations are making themselves heard on every side: we see groupings based on sex, on age (one of the most natural and yet most striking results of the gulf between the older and the younger generation caused by the War), on war-time experience, on religion, on economic interest and on professional occupation. All these, whatever ancestry may be claimed for them, are due to the democratic movement. For it is the extension of power from a privileged class to the body of the people which has made organization on the basis of common interest worth while.

The spread of democracy and of local and group thinking has exercised a further influence of which we are becoming daily more conscious. It has led to a great acceleration in the movement of public affairs, lessening the traditional lag between the promulgation of an idea and its

appearance as a practical political force. It was one of the
axioms of the old political science that ideas took ample
time to "grow and ripen," so that they could be carefully
watched and tended and, if necessary, pruned before they
became "practical politics." In England especially we
have been accustomed to think of political ideas and
institutions in terms of trees, not the scientifically regimented timber of a continental forest, but the spacious cen-
tury-old monarchs of the English park and countryside.
To-day we are forced to recognize that the metaphor does
not apply. Political ideas no longer grow in stillness: they
burst in upon us from near or far, often before we have
even been conscious that they had anywhere found minds
to lodge in. We have only to look back a generation and
consider the immense changes that have taken place—
changes almost greater in the other continents than in
the main scene of the Great War—to realize how completely calculations based on the older modes of reckoning
would be at fault to-day. When I was in Turkey in 1910
I remember Sir Edwin Pears, the *doyen* of the British
Colony at Constantinople, remarking to me that I would
live to see the Turk driven out of Salonica and how, Ox-
ford-trained as I was, I wondered whether he was not
over-sanguine. Who would have dared to predict that
within less than fifteen years the Caliphate itself would be
abolished? We must accustom ourselves to the fact that
the rhythm of public affairs has changed from an *andante*
to a *prestissimo*. Or, to vary the metaphor, we must
remember that we live in a world which is no longer leading a vegetative existence, but is pulsating with life and
equipped with an ever-increasing number of highly
charged nerve-centres.

One last condition of present-day political life must be

mentioned. The units of government to-day are not only smaller on the whole than they used to be, but also poorer. The War was carried on by States, not by private interests, and it is States that have to pay for it. The result has been the impoverishment of public power and an increase in its dependence upon private power. This is a condition which is already leading, and will lead increasingly, to serious consequences. One of them is the lessened attractiveness of the public service in its numerous fields—administrative, parliamentary and, most serious perhaps of all, judicial. Public life as a career had already begun to suffer from the fact that its framework is more limited than that of large-scale business. This does not come home to us so vividly in England as it does in the parliaments and government offices of the large majority of States; but it is true even of the greatest. If Wall Street offers more scope for an enterprising young man than Washington, and the City than Whitehall, where are we to expect statesmanlike talent to flow when it springs up in communities of smaller calibre? Even Geneva itself, with its world-wide outlook and possibilities of action, has proved too humdrum for some aspiring spirits. Public life with its inevitable restrictions and its limited material rewards, with its endless calls on patience and on the capacity to suffer fools gladly, has less and less to offer compared with the kingdoms opened out from the wind-swept mountain tops of private power.

Needless to say, these difficulties are greatly intensified under conditions where the controlling power is not only private but also alien. Chartered company government has always been open to strong objections, and the increasing political influence, even in some of the older European countries, of foreign commercial and financial interests, is a phenomenon that must cause anxiety to every thoughtful observer of post-War tendencies.

To sum up this brief survey of present-day political conditions, we find ourselves in a world of larger businesses and smaller States, of richer businesses and poorer States, of more efficient businesses and less efficient States, of more glorious businesses and less glorious States. What we are witnessing is a drift of interest away from politics, from governments, from interest in public affairs.

In the old days politics seemed to have such an unshakable hold over men's minds that it was not uncommon to hear complaints that its rewards in prestige were excessive. Why, it would be asked, should the streets of our capital cities be filled with statues of statesmen, to the comparative neglect of the thinkers, artists and musicians? To-day, when statesmanship has become at once more difficult and more thankless, no one would wish to weaken one of the not very numerous inducements which still remain to the career of public service.

The decline in the power of governments and parliaments has produced another phenomenon which might at first sight seem inconsistent with what has just been said— the emergence of personal rule in certain countries where the parliamentary system has never struck deep roots. It is a mistake to regard these so-called dictatorships as representing in any sense an advance in the art of government: no one familiar with the permanent conditions of public life in the countries concerned would seriously make this claim. Their real psychological origin is very different: they represent an attempt on the part of a weak political organization, conscious that power is slipping from its grasp, to recapture and conserve what it can. This is not the place in which to pass judgment on the peoples who have adopted this expedient, or acquiesced in its adoption by energetic leaders over their head. No outsider can estimate whether the crisis in their public life was really such as to justify these stringent measures of self-protection, or whether the measures themselves will prove successful. But what is abundantly clear is that the parliaments and other traditional institutions which have been displaced were not able to solve, hardly even able satisfactorily to discuss, the real problems affecting their peoples. The power had slipped from them and was else-where—in some mysterious upper region of international organization into which national parliamentarians cannot penetrate. When even in Great Britain the country can be practically committed to so far-reaching a decision as the restoration of the gold standard behind the back of the Mother of Parliaments, how can we expect the prestige of younger bodies to survive intact in an age when the real problems are not such as they are equipped to grapple with?

Looked at from this point of view, the post-War dictatorships are not, as they seem at first sight, mere usurpations of domestic power: rather they represent an almost desperate effort to break out of the vicious circle of parochial politics and to grapple with the real problems affecting their countries.

This is perhaps more easily discerned from Geneva than from London. From the standpoint of international or-ganization it is always more convenient, other things being equal, to deal with a country under a dictatorship than to negotiate with the representative of a more complex form of government: for, once the Chief is persuaded, success for any project is assured. As Demosthenes said long ago, it is easier to do business with Philip than with the Athen-ian democracy. Thus, as we shall see in greater detail later on, by an irony arising out of the very character of public affairs, the League of Nations, which in the mind of President Wilson was to entrench democracy, if it has not actually weakened it, has certainly helped to make its existing weakness more manifest.

We conclude, then, that there is urgent need for institutions such as will enable the public power to retain or recover control over private interest.

The institutions for which we are seeking must, if the foregoing analysis is accepted, conform to three main conditions:

They must be able to operate effectively in the international as well as in the national domain.

They must be responsive to the control of local centres of power.

They must be capable of rapid adjustment to changing circumstances.

The bare enumeration is sufficient to make it clear that we are concerned with institutions of an entirely new type. Each of the three conditions stated involves the elimination of a cherished tradition in political thinking.

The first involves the elimination of the idea of absolute sovereignty.

The second involves the elimination of the idea of progress through increasing centralization.

The third involves the elimination of the idea of a system of checks and balances designed to ensure stability against the danger of too rapid change.

A few words may be added under each of these heads.

Political institutions designed to function internationally are necessarily designed to function in a world of other States. In other words, they are designed for purposes of co-operation, and of a co-operation which is not occasional and spasmodic, but regular and permanent. It is, of course, possible to maintain, in a technical sense, that absolute sovereignty can be preserved unimpaired in a co-operative system, that a group of absolute sovereigns can, without loss of their attributes, individually agree each temporarily to forego the necessary degree of absolute power in order to carry out the common purposes upon which they have each, in their sovereign will, agreed. But this kind of reasoning will convince no one, or at least no Englishman. The broad fact remains that sovereignty and co-operation are antithetical conceptions, representing antithetical tendencies. Sovereignty is a conception applicable to a world of self-contained units. Co-operation is a conception applicable to a world of interdependent groups. Sovereignty faces inward and marshals its forces against "the foreigner"—an unanalysed indistinguishable mass looming outside its own sharply marked borders. Co-operation looks outward, and transforms what has been strange and "foreign" into elements of working collaboration for recognized common interests. Thus in an interdependent world the term sovereignty, with its picturesque ancestry of "Great Monarchs," is silently dropping out. It will be an interesting study to watch its desuetude. Already it is less familiar in the world of affairs than in the world of the study; but it still survives on the lips of plenipotentiaries, not indeed in its old magnificence, but as a last resort in a difficult argument when their instructions forbid them to give way.

To accept the control of local centres of power in an interdependent world is to run counter to the whole hitherto accepted scheme of the development of political institutions. That scheme has been based on the idea of the steady expansion of areas of government. Progress, so we learned in the books, consisted in the advance from the

Tribe to the City, from the City to the Territorial State, from the Territorial State to the Empire, and thus, at some undefined future date, always placed many generations ahead, to the world as a single unit of government. Examined in detail, the scheme presents itself as a development of federalism, of a system of government, that is, which, however complex in detail, places the ultimate control in a single centre. Federalism means central control, or it means nothing.

But democracy, as we are now beginning to realize, dislikes large-scale units of government, whether federal or unitary. They are indeed open to many objections, of which the difficulty of maintaining a genuine system of party government is not the least. On the other hand, they undoubtedly make for a certain efficiency. The Balkans would be more efficiently governed to-day under the system designed by the German protagonists of Berlin-Baghdad than they are under their own independent governments. But, for good or for ill, the choice is not open to us. For the time being at any rate, while democracy is in the ascendant, we have reached the limits of the federal and centralizing tendency and are witnessing a turn of the tide towards local independence. It seems safe to say that there will never be a larger federation than the United States; and even there the difficulty of compressing all the complex interests of so vast a territory into a single channel is proving increasingly embarrassing both to the American and to other governments.

We must look forward, then, in the coming age to a steady increase in the membership of the society of States —an increase, that is, in the number of centres which desire to retain the last word and final control in decisions of policy. The diffusion of responsibility thus involved is dis-

agreeable to the administrative mind; but, in the world of
to-day, with its life and variety, it is as inevitable as the
railway, the telegraph and the aeroplane, those symbols
of material uniformity which have unwittingly brought all
this diversity to light. Moreover, even from the purely
administrative point of view, it would seem that the old
conception of increasing centralization may have been
mistaken; for in the economic sphere, where democratic
forces were relatively powerless, the development has been
by no means along these simple and obvious lines. Experience has revealed the limits of the power that can be
efficiently exercised from a single office, and devices such
as the cartel or the interlocking directorate indicate that
the tendency towards co-operation is making its way in
what might have seemed an unpromising field. Even the
War, that supreme example of collective effort, though it
produced a Commander-in-Chief for the armies of four
Great Powers, led to no economic generalissimo; nor is
there any in sight to-day in the private field.

Thus there are respectable administrative arguments
for the maintenance and increase of local centres of control. The moral arguments are far stronger. But to these
we shall return.

The system of checks and balances, which is exemplified
in so many details of existing political institutions, dates
from the time when the course of affairs was slow enough
to make inaction in general an innocuous policy. In the
eighteenth-century world it was natural to consider stability as the chief desideratum in a political constitution.
Power was in the hands of a privileged minority, and self-
interest combined with a reasonable judgment on the
world's affairs caused it to look with a suspicious eye on
any proposals of change. Hence our constitutional tradi-

tions have a certain architectural quality. Power is enclosed in a castle behind moat and battlements, and before an intruding proposal can obtain entrance there are elaborate precautions to be taken and elaborate formalities to be observed. Complaints are often made, especially in countries with detailed written constitutions, that "politics," by which is meant the party system, prevent the consideration of urgent and overdue reforms. But the fault does not lie with the system of party government or with the individuals in control of it. The difficulty is a deeper one; it is that the whole mechanism of domestic legislation and, in some countries, of the conduct of "foreign relations" also, is designed on lines appropriate to the conditions of a past age. This is best seen when progress in spheres subject to these hampering restrictions is contrasted with the results achieved under freer conditions. It is, in fact, not "the politicians" who are at fault, but the institutions that they are compelled to work with. In an age of active public opinion, where persuasion and adjustment are the order of the day, they remain the victims of rigid rules of their ancestors' making.

Thus our three prerequisites—co-operation, local independence and flexibility—point to the development of institutions of an entirely new type. The older institutions worked through the issue of commands from the centre of authority to the subjects of sovereignty at the circumference. The newer will be designed to facilitate the transmission and elucidation of ideas and policies so that all those affected by them can participate in their discussion. For the older institutions the sovereign at the centre was the driving force: for the newer the driving force is opinion, which is gathered up and diffused like electric power throughout all the living centres of the community. The older institutions are typified in the centurion who, in our modern age, does not even need to say "go," but merely signs a paper or presses a button; the newer are typified in the diplomat or, if you will, the teacher, the public servant whose function it is to explain and to persuade, if need be, to rebuke—in a word, to stand between opposing opinions and to bring them closer together for practical ends. Under the older dispensation it used to be said that "influence is not government." To-day influence has become not the whole but almost the whole of such central government and power of decision as the world will ever possess. The work of the world is, in fact, being carried on to-day by influence, that is, by persuasion and goodwill and the effort at understanding, by all the various processes which appeal patiently and honestly to men's minds and seek to bring home to them the opinions and desires and needs of their fellowmen in regions and circumstances remote from their own.

Thus far our discussion has been mainly theoretical. We have been setting forth the kind of institutions which ought to exist under present-day conditions. Let us now turn to see what institutions do actually exist to deal with public affairs in the world before our eyes. We shall find that, in spite of traditions and appearances, the misfit between public business and the institutions through which it is conducted is not so great as our analysis might lead us to suppose. For the movement of life and the tide of affairs cannot be restrained by formal barriers, and power finds its way past every obstacle to the place where working policies are actually thought out and laid down.

During the last decade, in fact, a whole new set of institutions has been silently growing up on lines corresponding to the needs of the age. They have been little

analysed, or even discussed, as yet, because the men engaged in using and developing them have little leisure to
explain their working or even perhaps to make clear to
their own minds how completely they contradict the traditional doctrines of political science.

The two most prominent examples of post-War political
institutions are the British Commonwealth and the League
of Nations.

The British Commonwealth is held together to-day by
influence, not by command. In fact, as we all know, this
has been the case for many years past, but it was only at
the Imperial Conference of 1926 that it was formally
placed on record. We hardly realize what a tremendous
venture of faith the decisions of that Conference involve,
or what a revolution in hitherto accepted canons of
political practice. "To propose that Great Britain should
voluntarily give up all authority over her colonies, . . ."
wrote Adam Smith,[1] "would be to propose such a measure
as never was and never will be adopted by any nation in
the world. . . . . The most visionary enthusiast would
scarce be capable of proposing such a measure, with any
serious hopes at least of its ever being adopted." Yet
adopted it has been, and not by a nation addicted to
visionary enthusiasm or romantic gestures, but by a
Conservative Government among a people distinguished
for practical sense and dislike of fine phrases.

From the purely formal point of view the Imperial Conference of 1926 denotes a surrender of power, probably the
greatest surrender of power ever made by any government
at any single moment. But, in the light of political reality,
it represents a leap forward in the organization of the
British Commonwealth from an eighteenth-century to a

[1] *Wealth of Nations*, Book IV, chap. vii, part 3, p.198 (Clarendon Press, 1869).

twentieth-century system. Thanks to the flexibility of our constitutional arrangements and to the fact that we are not burdened by a written constitution, we have been able to run right past some of our neighbours whose institutions are of far more recent date than our own. We need only consider the procedure which would have been needed in the United States to bring about changes analogous to those made so simply and easily in our own case last year.

To analyse the present-day working of the British Commonwealth and to compare it with the other great example of a post-War political institution, the League of Nations, would be a fascinating study. There is no time to develop the theme here. Suffice it to say that, while the League of Nations is the hub or central nerve-centre of a world-wide system of co-operation, the British Commonwealth succeeds in maintaining itself upon a co-operative basis without any central working institutions at all. Geneva is an office which is becoming a symbol. The British Commonwealth has no central office. It has a symbol—the Crown—but the Crown is independent of place. It belongs equally to all parts of the Commonwealth, and there is no difference between its status in the older nations and in the younger. Geneva is a capital city —a metropolis of a new kind, no doubt, requiring no array of government buildings but only two relatively modest offices, but nevertheless a metropolis. London is no longer a metropolis. It ranks with Ottawa and Dublin and Canberra. For many it is, and will always remain, a shrine. But that is something different.

To explain why the British Commonwealth can thus dispense with a centre would carry us too far into the realm of the unseen and imponderable. We all know that without a common outlook, common habits and common aims, the system as we know it would not work for a day. This is sufficient to suggest what a problem is involved in the promotion of a common outlook, common habits and common aims in a newly-established co-operative system whose members do not set out with these advantages This is the task which is being undertaken at Geneva.

The League of Nations has been neatly defined, by one of those who know it best, as "the maximum of co-opera-tion between governments at any given moment." The definition is characteristic in its elusiveness. It does not attempt to tell you what the League of Nations is or does. It merely situates it in its relationship to other bodies. We are far removed here from the old world of absolute powers and rights: instead, we find ourselves in a relativistic universe where everything is measured by something else and the whole world, with everything in it, is moving and changing all the time. The League of Nations, in fact, has no fixed powers and attributes. It may be much to-day and little or almost nothing to-morrow. It is not a government but a contrivance for adjustment between governments, not a State but a table at which States sit down to do business. You can bring States to a table, but you cannot make them agree, as the League authorities, and all the world, realized with a shock in March 1926. A co-operative system provides no specific, except goodwill and good sense, against deadlock and dissolution. Nevertheless, the existence of the table is a powerful incentive to agreement. There is a school of psychology which maintains that the physical gesture precedes and calls up the sensation it de-notes—that men are ashamed because they blush and afraid because they turn pale. In the same way it may be said, and in this case there is ample experience to bear it out, that to provide the physical prerequisites of agreement is to have gone a considerable way towards its attainment.

But who sits at the table? Who are the human agents by whom this co-operative system is carried on? It is here that we come to the heart of the subject. The system by which the chairs at this metaphysical table are filled or, in other words, the principles underlying this new experiment in international consultation and administration, have been set out in exemplary fashion in the best book, in my humble judgment, that has as yet been written about the League. It does not mention the League in its title, and hence you will not find it in the bibliographies. It is called *Allied Shipping Control*,[1] and professes to deal with what is called on the title-page, "an experiment in international administration." But in a concluding portion the author, Sir Arthur Salter, sums up and develops the lessons of the experience gained in that maximum degree of co-operation between the Allied governments which characterized the last year of the War; and, in fact, those lessons have been put into practice at Geneva and have formed the basis of the work of the technical organizations of the League.

"The institution of the League of Nations, with its principles of publicity and open diplomacy," writes Sir Arthur Salter, "is an attempt to take public policy away from the few overstrained centres of excessive power, and to base it boldly and broadly on the general wishes and will of the peoples of the world. It is morally a great effort of faith. It is, in one sense, administratively a great effort of decentralization. It replaces centralization by co-ordination."

[1]Oxford University Press, 1921. (*Economic and Social History of the World War, British Series.*)

This is not the place in which to develop in detail the reasoning in which this thesis is expounded. It is to be hoped that the head of the Financial and Economic Section of the League will himself be persuaded to expand into a book, illuminated by his experience during the last few years, his own brief outline sketch. For our present purpose it is enough to draw attention to two aspects of the League's procedure in "taking public policy away from the few overstrained centres of excessive power." It has brought to the table both new subjects of international discussion and new types of men to deal with them.

Let us look first at the men. Geneva delegates may be divided into five classes: (1) responsible Ministers; (2) the men whom Sir Arthur Salter describes as the "crucial officers" of government departments, that is to say, those who draw up and submit to the responsible Minister the policies on their particular subjects; (3) *ad hoc* government delegates, nominated for a particular conference or other occasion; (4) non-governmental experts nominated by responsible international bodies, such for instance as the International Chamber of Commerce; (5) non-governmental experts nominated by the Council of the League of Nations.

Out of these only the first class and a certain proportion of the third embody persons engaged in what were known as "foreign affairs" before the War. The other classes, and part of the third, represent the recruitment into official international activity of personalities and capacities hitherto outside its orbit. The far-reaching significance of this extension of range will become clear to anyone who will take the trouble to compare the personnel engaged in pre-War international conferences and other official activities with the names enumerated in the recently published

Yearbook of the League.[1] What has, in fact, happened is that an increasing call is being made on the type of judgment and experience represented in Great Britain by the persons chosen to serve on Royal Commissions and similar bodies. But there is this important difference— that Royal Commissions perform the task required of them and dissolve, whereas the men who serve on League Commissions find themselves an integral part of a permanent organization with which they are kept closely in touch through their secretary, a regular official of the League.

Let us look now at the range of function which these new international Committees cover. Towards the end of the War a Committee of the short-lived Ministry of Reconstruction, of which Lord Haldane was the chairman and Mrs. Sidney Webb an active member, drew up a scientific scheme, based on a careful analysis of the functions of a modern government, for the redistribution of work among the various administrative departments. It is interesting to observe that the authorities of the League, working no doubt quite independently of any preconceived scheme, have developed an organization corresponding very closely, *mutatis mutandis*, to that then recommended for Great Britain. But keeping to the British system as it is, the various activities of the League have brought to Geneva in the last few years representatives of the following Departments: the Treasury, the Foreign Office, the Home Office, the Colonial Office, the War Office, the India Office, the Admiralty, the Air Ministry, the Board of Trade, the Ministry of Health, the Board of Education, the Ministry of Transport and the

[1] *Annuaire de la Société des Nations*, edited by Georges Ottlik. Geneva: Payot. Second edition, 1928.

Post Office. There is hardly a single department of government, in fact, which has not developed an international extension, and many of them have been in such close and frequent contact with Geneva that the "crucial officer" may almost be described as engaged part-time on foreign service.

We are now in a position to appreciate the significance of this new technique of international co-operation surveyed as a whole. It represents the extension of the conception of public affairs, of "res publica," to correspond with the similar extension that has taken place in private affairs during the last few generations. Government has found itself outstripped by the development of modern society, which challenges its authority and diminishes its control. It has replied by developing an international political organization on the new and more serviceable model. But it has done more than that. It has looked for allies in spheres wider than those over which private power exercises its sway. It has summoned to its councils doctors, lawyers, engineers, agricultural experts, social workers and representatives of other professions and interests who have hitherto been remote from public affairs except in their capacity as plain citizens and voters. "Res publica," in other words, has called in new worlds to redress the balance weighed down by "res privata."

But it is going even further. It is facing the problem, which, as we have seen, was set on one side during the nineteenth century, of breaking down the division between public and private, between the political and the economic, by working out an effective and organic relationship between the two spheres. The development of the economic organs of the League and of its relationship with professional bodies in the economic sphere, such as the

International Chamber of Commerce and the International Federation of Trade Unions, forms in itself a striking example of the new system of international co-operation which deserves to have its history written in detail. Here it is sufficient to point, without further analysis, to the four new organs that have come into existence since 1918—the Economic Committee, the Financial Committee, the Consultative Committee which is being set up as a result of the World Economic Conference, and the International Labour Office with a governing body composed of representatives of governments, employers' organizations and trade unions. Their existence is a witness to the fact that the new conditions have changed the outlook in the economic world as well as in the political. If they have compelled governments to think internationally, they have also compelled business men to think in terms of public service. They have turned bankers, manufacturers, traders and trade union leaders into statesmen—into persons engaged on work of a public character and involving public responsibility.

But the integration between political and economic institutions is not yet by any means complete. We are, in fact, in the midst of a development which is going on very rapidly and without sufficient account being taken of its broader bearings. There is a field here for study and for practical suggestion which opens out, as it seems to me, an opportunity for the special activity of the Royal Institute.

Take two examples illustrating the present state of the relations between the public and the private system.

At about the same time that the League of Nations collected at Geneva some two hundred delegates to confer in public on the economic affairs of the world, four men met privately in a room in New York. They were the Governor

of the Bank of England, the Governor of the Federal
Reserve Bank of New York, the Governor of the Bank of
Germany and the Deputy-Governor of the Bank of
France. They met behind closed doors and no report was
issued of their deliberations. Yet their decisions, within
their own extremely important range, were of greater
practical effect for the economic life of the world than
those of the conference at Geneva. But the men that
framed them have no constitutional responsibility. If they
render a stewardship it is not to their peoples but to their
shareholders. Their business was public business in the
fullest sense of the word, and they discussed it, we need
have no doubt, in the spirit of statesmen. But they were
statesmen working without the institutions appropriate
for statesmanlike work.

I read in *The Times* of this very morning that "it is no
exaggeration to say that the economic reconstruction of
Europe owes more to the Governor of the Bank of England
than to any other single person."[1] Is the economic reconstruction of Europe a matter for statesmanship or for
private business? If it is statesmanship, does not the very
tribute suggest reflections on the constitutional position of
the statesman? Do we not need new institutions, or new
adaptations of existing institutions, which will bring appearances into rather more correspondence with realities?

Take again, as a second example, the Dawes Plan.
Surely the history of the Dawes Plan represents a very
striking innovation in international affairs. A body of
private persons makes a report on a problem which has
been tormenting the public life of Europe for half a decade. The report is drawn up with so much knowledge and
judgment, it is so admirably adapted to the needs of the

---

[1] *The Times*, November 8th, 1927—*City Supplement*, p. xv.

time, that it is accepted *en bloc* by the governments and peoples concerned and has become one of the main elements in the international political system of the years through which we are passing. Yet the men who drew it up were not finance ministers or departmental officials. They were private individuals, chosen just because they had a breadth of outlook, a detachment, and perhaps also a range of knowledge, not commonly found in governmental circles.

A similar instance in a more limited sphere is the influence which is being increasingly exercised by the annual statements of the leading British banking authorities. These pronouncements are composed with a greater sense of public responsibility and studied with greater attention than much of what is said by members of Parliament or even Ministers. They have become important political events. Yet they are not delivered in Parliament or before any publicly constituted assembly, but at shareholders' meetings.

It would be an interesting study to trace how, in the comparatively few years that have elapsed since the end of the War, opinion in the economic world has been, as it were, politicized, driven by the force of events to adopt a statesmanlike attitude towards public affairs. It would show opinion passing, in the international domain, through the whole gamut traversed during the nineteenth century in regard to national governments. The *laissez-faire* outburst after the Armistice corresponds to the violent resentment against governments and their abuses which characterized the eighteenth and early nineteenth century reformers. Then there came a growing appreciation that there was a use for government in the international sphere, if only for police purposes. Then came the recognition of the idea of international government in what may be called the sphere of social reform, as an instrument for securing fair dealing between country and country, and sweeping away unjust discriminations. This is on the whole the political philosophy pervading the deliberations of the Economic Conference. Finally, there is an increasing recognition that, in the international sphere as in the national, there is room for genuine and effective co-operation between economic and political power, not simply to redress recognized abuses but to promote positive common aims and projects. This is the stage upon which we are just beginning to enter, and its possibilities of fruitful action are limitless. It is characteristic of the acceleration in the pace of present-day movements that a development which took well-nigh a century on the narrower stage should have taken less than a decade on the larger.

I turn now to another significant development in collective organization which has been developed less far at present than those to which I have referred, but holds out even greater possibilities for the future. I refer to the collaboration of the world of thought, the scholars, the writers, the artists and the educators, with the world of action. After all, the great transformation of the modern world that is responsible for the international problems of to-day is the work of modern science. It was due to lonely thinkers in their studies and laboratories. Has science nothing to say as to the use made of her discoveries? Clearly, in a world of advisory committees and professional organization, in which every section of the community is finding means to express its views and exercise influence through the processes of persuasion, those whose special function it is to reflect and create rather than to command are naturally called upon to come into their own. This is the idea behind what is called, in a term which has misleading associations in England, international intellectual co-operation.

Thus far we have been surveying the development of political institutions since the War as a process of mobilizing experts to recover control over private power. There has been a kind of counter-demonstration of efficiency on the part of public power against a competitor that had outstripped it. Seen from this angle the League takes on the appearance of a complex interlocking system of advisory Committees designed to supervise the interlocking directorates which have contributed so much to the efficiency and flexibility of private power. A public bureaucracy, of a new kind, has been brought into existence to keep watch over the new model of private bureaucracy.

Here, after what must have seemed a long *détour*, we are brought sharply back to the problem from which we started. Where, amid these contending bureaucracies, in this play of experts and professionals, are we to look for democracy? What place is there for the plain man in an internationally organized world? Are not its problems too difficult, too complex, too large in scale, for him to grapple with? Are not the real political problems of to-day being settled, in fact, altogether over his head? Is he not being treated in international affairs with much the same scornful indifference as that to which he is being exposed in domestic affairs by dictators in certain countries? Has not democracy as an effective political system outlived its usefulness?

The conclusion seems obvious and even tempting, and has received powerful and unexpected support even in "progressive" quarters. But those who encourage or acquiesce in it have overlooked one crucial factor. Democracy may be powerless to govern; but it is still strong enough to interfere decisively in the conduct of government by others. Inapt for constructive tasks, it can still wield the weapon of *sabotage*. "The House of Commons," an international official remarked to me recently, "has drifted today into much the same position as that of the monarch some two centuries ago. It has nothing left but the power of veto." The statement is an obvious exaggeration; but, even if it were true, the veto by itself is a power not to be despised. The influence of popular and parliamentary opinion, so far from having been negligible, has in fact been a dominant factor in international affairs ever since the cessation of hostilities. Over and over again the plans of the experts and the desires of the statesmen have been thwarted by the resolute negative of the peoples. For us in Europe the most familiar and irritating example is the fixed attitude of the bulk of the American electorate on the question of inter-governmental debts. But electorates in the various European countries have insisted on policies quite as difficult for the plain man on the other side of the Atlantic to understand. The power of popular veto is a fact which cannot be ruled out or wished away. The Roman Empire developed a system of government which drained off power and responsibility from the common man until it perished from his inanition. For good or for evil we are exempt from this temptation to pave the way for invading barbarians. Our barbarians are already within the gates and they are very much alive. We have taught them to be skilled producers in the new interdependent economic system and have established schools which enable them to do their tasks efficiently. Compulsory education is inseparable, in the long run, from popular government.

Those who, in the various industrial countries, in the nine-teenth century, enabled the people to read and write were giving hostages to democracy which the few can never recover. Thus the issue which we have to face is not whether the common man is or is not to have a share in government. It is whether his share is to be an unhelpful participation in a clumsy system of checks and balances, or an allocation corresponding to the special contribution he is fitted to make.

Political democracy then, even in the large-scale post-War world, is, in the advanced countries, and will in-creasingly be elsewhere, not a matter of choice but a mat-ter of necessity. But far be it from me to represent it as a mere *pis aller*. It is also, of course, a moral agency of the highest value. If I refrain from emphasizing this in detail it is not out of forgetfulness or indifference, but because I assume that in England it is not necessary to recapitulate accepted doctrines. In the matter of the moral values of popular government we stand on the shoulders of the Victorians. I need do no more than recall one sentence from Mill which states the issue succinctly and recalls the whole world of this argument. " *There cannot*," he says in a famous chapter of his *Political Economy*,[1] "*be a combina-tion of circumstances more dangerous to human welfare, than that in which intelligence and talent are maintained at a high standard within a governing corporation, but starved and discouraged outside the pale.*" Here, stated in a sentence, is the reason why we cannot leave the plain man outside the League of Nations.

We need then to relate the electorate to the practical realities of the post-War world. We need to broaden the whole framework in which the national democracies do

[1] Book V, chap. xi, § 6. (London: Longmans, 1909.)

their business. We need to develop the new agencies of "liaison" and interpretation until they extend their influence right down to the common man and woman. That, as I see it, is the problem of democracy to-day, the problem on the solution of which its survival as an effective governing force depends. That is the field which post-War developments in government call us urgently to explore.

To devise the means by which the common man may be enabled to play a useful and effective part in government under the new conditions of the post-War world is the chief political task of our generation; for it is upon this that the future of government, in the traditional British sense of the word, depends. We have, in fact, arrived at a decisive turning-point in the development of the art of government. If we can develop political institutions so as to adjust the democratic svstem. as it has grown up in the more limited pre-War world, to the new international situation, we can look forward confidently to the future of constitutional government and of the rule of law in the world's affairs. But if the gulf between democracy and government, between the common man and the conduct of public affairs, is allowed to widen, it is not political democracy alone which will disappear. It is constitutional government itself, with all the wealth of tradition and of inherited wisdom which it embodies. For, without the support of public opinion and the power of public control behind it the new Civil Service, as we may call it, however devoted its service and however extended its range, will not in the long run be able to hold its own against the encroachments of private interest. The greatest weapon of the League, as has been shown time after time, is publicity. But what is the value of publicity when there is no more public? A Civil Service cannot function except in a society of citizens.

How is the elector to be brought more closely into touch with public affairs, so that political democracy may once more become a reality? I have no intention of wearying you with a programme. The subject is much too vast and too difficult for cursory treatment; for it involves nothing less than a re-survey of our existing institutions from a new angle. All that I can do is to indicate certain general directions in which progress is to be looked for, leaving it to those who have a closer knowledge than I of the conditions in each domain to carry the inquiry further.

But first it may be well to make one general observation. Political democracy will never be a reality until we have broken down the distinction that has grown up in our minds and in customary speech between "party politics" and serious political thinking. The extension of the electorate and the increased frivolity of the daily Press have led us to think of "party politics" as a kind of rough-and-tumble contest into which we cast certain selected issues, judged suitable to exercise the energies of rival groups of players. To keep an issue out of party politics is to reserve it for serious consideration; to admit it to the *mêlée* is to subject it to every kind of distortion; and men who under ordinary circumstances attend to public business with judicial calm and unswerving intellectual integrity consider themselves justified in throwing their political quality to the winds in tasting the joys of the party struggle. "The Briton," said the Prime Minister recently in a debate worthy of the best traditions of the House of Commons, "owing to his training, his character, his history, has one rare gift . . . that when he finds himself acting in a judicial capacity he can bring an unbiassed mind to the discharge of his duties and *dissociate himself from all the external paraphernalia of controversy in which we take so much delight on the floor of this Chamber.*"[1] The people have a right to demand from their representatives that the "unbiassed mind" shall not be treated as a rarity to be brought out for use on special occasions when the "paraphernalia" are set aside and the great game is temporarily in abeyance, but shall be kept in use for all the ordinary tasks which the country sets for its public men.

Let me briefly indicate six directions in which help may be sought.

The first is the field of education. We have hardly yet begun to realize the kind of education needed in a truly democratic community. "Self-determination," if it is to be carried through in this sphere without disastrous anarchy, involves a community of human beings who have a reasonable degree of choice and freedom as regards their own occupation and also some general understanding of the world in which they live. Translated into concrete terms, this means a large increase in the facilities available for the younger generation among the poorer classes, and a corresponding improvement in the quality of what is offered. Much of the State-supported education provided in various European countries to-day still represents a survival from the time when it was introduced as an inferior variety side by side with the traditional facilities provided for the *élite*. To develop this point further would carry us too far. It is enough to point out that the work of the elementary teacher is as important and as difficult as that at any other stage of education, and that one of the

[1]*House of Commons Debates*, November 25th, 1927. [The quotation is so apt for my argument that, although it occurs in a speech delivered later than my address, I embodied it when writing out my notes.]

best ways of democratizing education, in the true sense of the term, is to promote a sense of the unity and dignity of the profession in all its activities. Scotland and the Scandinavian countries have already pointed the way in this direction.

Another field in which we are only just beginning to realize the possibilities is that of so-called adult education. If the common man is to exercise his judgment on public affairs he must have access to the means for forming it. Newspapers are not enough: he needs access to books, and expensive books. The rise in the cost of printing has not only made it more difficult for students to procure the best new books in their own country; it is acting as a serious obstacle to the spread of new and valuable ideas across national frontiers. One of the real needs of the day is the establishment of an international lending library, on the model of the London Library, with the object of bringing newly-published foreign books to the homes of readers of modest means. A practical scheme of this sort would do more to lay the basis of an international public opinion than a great deal of more loudly-heralded propaganda.

Another means through which public opinion could be formed and guided is through the establishment of a regular relationship between the world of thought and the world of action. Whence does the common man at present derive his opinions? Partly out of his own experience, partly from the opinions of others. But these others are generally by no means those best qualified to express them. Modern civilization has not yet discovered how to assign the proper value to what is first-class in the intellectual sphere. It is recognized in its own domain; but the modesty of the truly great exposes them to an unequal competition with mediocrity better versed in the art of advertisement.

It is easy to smile at academies. Nevertheless, there is a certain dignity attaching to the leaders in the world of thought and beauty which it is to the advantage of democracy to uphold. It is to them that public opinion ought naturally to turn for advice on a whole realm of questions which are at present hardly being attended to, because they are the concern of nobody in particular.

In a striking passage of his memoirs Lord Grey, in a phrase that is often quoted, speaks of "events" as having a "mind" of their own. The words embody an honest confession that he and his colleagues were unable to stem the tide of the forces amid which they found themselves. Lord Grey is no materialist; but he is driven to admit, for one crucial episode at any rate, the impotence of human direction for the control of the blind interaction of contending human purposes which we call "events." Can we recover such a power of direction? It is too early to answer, for we have never tried. But at least we can analyse the problem and see that it is discussed by the minds best qualified to pass judgment on it. Is civilization holding its own against the forces of barbarism within and without? Is the intellectual and artistic life of the world, for instance, being unduly commercialized? Is freedom of thought and expression less widespread, and less assured, than a generation or two ago? Is specialization exercising a baneful effect on intellectual life? Is the application of mechanical methods and inventions to the sphere of art leading to a lowering of its finer standards? All these are large yet definite questions, much discussed in intimate gatherings, but never yet authoritatively set out and pressed home. In all these and similar matters the common man would respond to guidance. But at present he does not know where to turn for it.

I pass now from influences affecting the formation of public opinion to the domain of politics in the more familiar sense of the word.

Can the common man be brought to take an active interest in international problems? If by that is meant that he should follow them as closely and with as considered a judgment as he can and often does devote to domestic issues, the answer is clearly in the negative. The problems of the large-scale modern world are at once too intricate and too remote to command the sustained attention of the ordinary voter. Enlarge his vision and his opportunities for acquiring knowledge as you will, the detailed issues that form the staple of treaties and international conventions will never be as real to him as those that form the subject of legislation in national parliaments. Diplomacy will never be subjected to the same degree of popular control as more purely parochial concerns. "All that I know of India," a candid member of the House of Commons remarked to me many years ago, "is that I know nothing of India." Parliamentary control over Indian affairs has shown a marked increase since that apophthegm was uttered; but if for India we read Lithuania, or Tacna-Arica, or Tangier, or even questions of more general interest, such as the abolition of export prohibitions or the adoption of rules for a general most-favoured-nation system, there is no doubt that it represents the general public and even Parliamentary attitude. These are subjects which cannot easily be made electoral issues. One can go further and say that it is disastrous to try and make them so, for it would be to risk the revival of the atmosphere which characterized the discussion of particular issues of foreign policy in the days of Palmerston and Gladstone.

But, when all this is granted, there remains one aspect

of international politics on which public opinion can and should express itself directly and emphatically—the question of peace and war. It is for that reason that it has become perhaps the most urgent task of post-War democracy to devise means by which the problem of the prevention of war may be effectively detached and isolated from the more detailed and specialized issues of international politics. The chief value of the "test of aggression" and other proposals of the same kind designed to "outlaw" war is that they provide a practicable means for bringing an international public opinion to bear on the problem of peace and war. One might even say that they provide, for the first time, a means for bringing such a public opinion into existence at all.

We have described the League of Nations as a table at which the negotiators concede as much, in the way of international co-operation, as their local public opinion allows them. Here at last is an issue in which public opinion, so far from being a restraint, may be a powerful impelling force. The great weakness of the League, which comes out very clearly when it is compared with the British Commonwealth, is that it is too much of a mere mechanism, that it lacks the moral authority which constitutes the heart and reality of modern government. How can the League acquire moral authority? Not through the play of any of the influences which have made for political unity in a more limited sphere. The peoples members of the League will never share common intimate memories or let their thoughts and feelings run into common channels of literature and art like more close-knit national units. The League is not and cannot be based on a common culture. Only one idea is capable of binding it together, of becoming its symbol, and thus giving it the authority that it has hitherto lacked—the idea of Peace. It is Peace and Peace alone which can arm the League with the power to command in the one sphere of command which is left, and must always be left, to human government.

There are some wise words of Bagehot which have a valuable application for the League in the present stage of its development:

"No one can approach to an understanding of the English institutions, or of others, which, being the growth of many centuries, exercise a wide sway over mixed populations, unless he divide them into two classes. In such constitutions there are two parts . . . first, those which excite and preserve the reverence of the population—the *dignified* parts if I may so call them; and next, the *efficient* parts—those by which it, in fact, works and rules. There are two great objects which every constitution must attain to be successful, which every old and celebrated one must have wonderfully achieved: every constitution must first *gain* authority and then *use* authority; it must first win the loyalty and confidence of mankind, and then employ that homage in the work of government." [1]

The statesmen who meet at Geneva have it within their power so to define the problem of peace and war as to interest, indeed to create, an international public opinion regarding the rules and principles that the League has laid down. Once the League has achieved this, it will be found that it has gained an authority which it is then in a position to use. I have no intention of going into the details of the controversy regarding arbitration and security. My only concern with it here is to bring out the vital connection between political democracy and the effective organization of peace. The British Commonwealth has made war inconceivable between its independent members without prejudice to their perfect freedom in every other respect. The moral and political development of the League

[1] *The English Constitution*, p. 4 (ed. 1882).

of Nations can only be ensured on the same lines. The pro-
hibition of war is the most important prerequisite of post-
War democracy. Once the police-power of the League is
acknowledged, the world will have a framework of law
and government within which it can develop all that the
age demands of local independence and national diversity.
What the King's Peace did for England in the twelfth
century, before Parliament had come into being, the
League's Peace can do for the world in the twentieth.

It is perhaps worth adding that the establishment of
this framework, important as it is for the smaller States,
is of quite exceptional importance for the British Commonwealth. For a world-wide political community based on
local centres of power assured peace is a vital need; for
war in any part of the world would awaken conflicts of
interest and policy which would make it very difficult to
preserve unity of action. Moreover, the real storm-centre
of international politics to-day is not Europe, but the
Pacific. Thus the present situation, in which one part of
the British Commonwealth is pledged to use its police-
power in one, and not the most menacing danger-zone,
represents an uncomfortable transition stage. It has re-
opened the problem of the unity of the British Commonwealth in time of war without bringing a clear set of rules
to bear upon it from the side of the League. Thus it is a
specific British interest as well as a general interest of
democracy to hasten the development of international
police-power.

But if there is only one domain in which the whole of
international public opinion can be mobilized, there is no
reason why *some* international public opinion should not
be mobilized in every domain. The duty of a citizen in the
modern world is not to know everything about every-

thing; but we may well demand of him that he should know something of everything and everything of something. In point of fact this is what is actually happening through the development of specialization and of professional organization. It has already been pointed out how international problems have become specialized through being distributed among individual government departments and how a system of expert collaboration has been developed with non-official bodies. What is needed to ensure a healthy flow of public opinion in each domain is simply that these bodies themselves should be in touch with the individual citizens in each country whose work lies in this special field.

In the economic field this organization already exists to a large extent. The banker, the business man and the workman can, if they desire, keep in touch with international problems in their field through the organizations created for that purpose. The same development is taking place in regard to other professions. As the international bearings of the issues arising in each field become more apparent, men will turn more and more to the new institutions set up to deal with them, and the democratic possibilities opened out by the existence of international advisory bodies over the whole range of public affairs will be better understood.

Here again progress depends on persuading the individual citizen to take a broader view of what constitutes "politics." To the Athenians, who originated the idea of democracy, popular government meant, before all things, personal service. When the modern citizen realizes that his voting power is only one, and not the most important part, of his political responsibility and that the community relies on him as an element in a healthy public opinion to exercise his judgment on the issues of his specialty or occupation, democracy will be on a far firmer basis than that made for it by the eighteenth and nineteenth century theorists. Knowledge is Power: and the only way to counteract the oligarchy of the controlling Few in each domain is to mobilize the knowledge of the Many who have sufficient professional attainments to call them to account.

There is a fifth direction in which we must look for the strengthening of political democracy—the rehabilitation of parliaments.

Parliaments, or Chambers of Deputies, as we know them, are a survival from the time when their members were legislators. To-day, as we have seen, some of the most important issues are international and form the subject of international treaties or conventions, which may or may not be subject to ratification, but are seldom subject to amendment, by national parliaments. But even domestic legislation is, as a rule, not framed by the so-called legislators. It issues from the expert Departments, sometimes after consultation with the representatives of the interests concerned. This procedure, which is perfectly legitimate and even natural, results from the complexity of modern life, which prevents even the chosen representatives of the people from knowing everything about everything.

What then is the deputy to do? What place is left for him? If he does not make laws, what other function can he fulfil, beyond registering the decrees of the executive?

The fact is that the position and functions of a parliamentarian under modern conditions have not been subjected to sufficient analysis; and this has placed him in a false position which is responsible for much of the *malaise* in the parliamentary atmosphere of to-day. We need a clearer definition of the relationship between the specialist bodies, which alone are competent to frame technical bills, and the representatives of the general national interest.

A deputy under modern conditions has two main functions. The first is to bring his general knowledge and common sense and responsibility for the public interest to bear on every problem whatsoever that arises in public affairs—to form part of the "grand inquest" of the nation. How far this general control should be exercised through special committees devoted to receiving reports or listening to testimonies from the expert administrators or the representatives of advisory bodies is a matter which every national parliament must decide for itself; but it might well form the subject of an inquiry by this Institute. There is a hiatus at present between the deputy and the expert, between the working member of the House of Commons and the official who works out the national policy and represents it at international conferences, which certainly leaves something to be desired. The constitutional monarch, even though he has lost his veto, still retains the right to be completely informed on every subject. Parliaments which retain the veto should have every facility, written and oral, that is necessary for its effective exercise.[1]

The second function of the parliamentarian is to educate the voters. This may seem a paradoxical way of stating the relationship between the Sovereign people and the object of their confidence; but in fact it is precisely the bestowal of this confidence which enables them to be educators. Some of the finest experiments in adult educa-

[1] See Appendix II.

tion have been those embodied in the relationship of men like Morley and Bryce with their Scottish constituents. Electioneering has not indeed a very respectable history in most countries, including our own with its memories of the hustings; and it is too often conducted to-day with an eye to the least public-spirited section of the electorate, that last ten per cent, who have to be driven to the poll by raging, tearing propaganda. In the short run such methods are sometimes, but not always, successful; but, even in electoral methods, it is the long distance that counts. The member or candidate who regards it as his duty to keep his constituents abreast of the problems of the day, in their national and international, as well as their local bearings, is not only rendering a service to democracy which no one else is in an equal position to perform, but is consolidating his own position with all those—and they are very numerous in every constituency—who have a real appreciation of the qualities that go to make a good representative. A parliament so composed would act as a real agency of transmission and interpretation between the expert and the common man and between the international and the local.

The position of members of this type would be greatly strengthened if an improvement were made in the economic basis of their profession. I use the expression advisedly, for to be a representative is as much a whole-time and professional task as to be a Civil servant. One reason for the decline of parliaments is that they do not provide a career with prospects sufficient to attract the ability and public spirit which are drawn into the Civil Service and, increasingly, into private business. When so many inquiries are being instituted into the economic basis of other occupations, the question of how to ensure that the central profession in the community is adequately recruited might well be investigated. It is not easy to provide security for the members of a profession exposed to electoral vicissitudes; but some approximation to it may be found, at least in favour of those who have so far succeeded in it as to have risen to office or to the Front Bench. In any case it is idle to lament the inevitable decline of parliamentarism so long as no effort has been made to improve the conditions and prospects of parliamentary work.

A sixth and last direction in which a change for the better can be looked for is through what I would call the "de-specialization of the expert." The expert, like the common man, should know something about everything as well as everything about something, and he should be under the further obligation of being able to explain the bearings of his own specialism on the public welfare. We have reached a point in the accumulation of knowledge and the development of civilization when we need to re-knit the links between the specialist and the world of knowledge for which he is working. There is such a thing as a parliament of thought; but in that parliament the members should not be distinct from the experts, as is the case in the world of action, but each of them should have a constant sense of his own place in relation to the whole. When "expertise" comes to be associated in men's minds with the idea of synthesis as well as of analysis, it will have lost more than half its terror and another great stumbling-block to democracy, at least in the English-speaking world, will have been removed.

Democracy, as I have tried to present it, is something very different from the simple old doctrine of government of the people, for the people, by the people. It may be described, to adapt another phrase of Abraham Lincoln's, as "government of all the people some of the time and of some of the people all the time." It is a partnership between Science and Common Sense, between special knowledge and general experience, between life seen steadily from a single angle and life seen as a whole by the eye of the ubiquitous multitude. It is an association, precarious yet ever renewed, between all the many and varied groups that make up the sum of the world's opinion, an association only rendered possible by a constant process of passing the lamp.

And the lamp-bearers, the transmitters, the human agents through whom alone these new institutions of co-operation can function, where are we to look for them, or at least for their best exemplars, except in the country which has devised, in Dominion status, the world's first model of international co-operative institutions? Britain is the greatest existing reservoir of public spirit. Without that resource to draw on, the chances for democracy to survive the perils that beset it would be greatly weakened. Intelligence allied with public spirit is still, and will perhaps always remain, in a small minority among the mass of mankind. But a minority, with the moral forces on its side, can win through. If the democratic system survives and adjusts itself to the new conditions, it will not be because the majority of the world is ripe for it, but because economic forces compelled the world to choose between international government and private tyranny and no alternative political system was available. In that situation a minority of responsible peoples, acting together in association, must preserve the inherited traditions of government and pass them on to the less experienced.

That is the task of the League of Nations in the first period of its life; and that is the especial task of the peoples of the British Commonwealth, who bring to it their own unique experience of constitutional government and international co-operation.

# APPENDIX I

The best known example of politics breaking into an economic argument is Adam Smith's famous discussion of the Navigation Act in Book IV, chap. ii, of the *Wealth of Nations*. After proving conclusively that "the Act of navigation is not favourable to foreign commerce or to the growth of that opulence which can arise from it," he concludes the discussion with the well-known *obiter dictum:* "as defence, however, is of much more importance than opulence, the Act of Navigation is, perhaps, the wisest of all the commercial regulations of England." There is an even more curious instance of the intrusion of reality into an abstract discussion in Ricardo's chapter on Foreign Trade. He has been using the familiar argument that "under a system of perfectly free commerce, each country naturally devotes its capital and labour to such employments as are most beneficial to each," and that one of the benefits of this system is that "it distributes labour most effectively and economically." Nevertheless, a few paragraphs later he corrects his whole argument with the following observation:

"Experience, however, shows, that the fancied or real insecurity of capital, when not under the immediate control of its owner, together with the *natural disinclination which every man has to quit the country of his birth and connexions*, and intrust himself, with all his habits fixed, to a strange government and new laws, check the emigration of capital. These feelings, *which I should be sorry to see weakened*, induce most men of property to be satisfied with a low rate of profits in their own country, rather than seek a more advantageous employment for their wealth in foreign nations." [1]

[1] *The Works of David Ricardo, Esq., M.P.*, p. 77. (London: Murray, 1846.)

But the most interesting example, particularly in view of our present-day discussions on arbitration and security, is the discussion of the international regulation of blockade policy by Cobden in his speech of October 25th, 1862, during the American Civil War. It is worth quoting in full both on account of the importance of the subject (since echoes of Cobden's views on it are still to be heard in the British Press in spite of Article XVI of the Covenant) and also because it illustrates the extraordinary *naïveté* with which this hard-headed business man approaches the problem of the guarantees of international law:[1]

"With the general spread of Free-trade principles—by which I mean nothing but the principle of the division of labour carried over the whole world—one part of the earth must become more and more dependent upon another for the supply of its material and its food. Instead of, as formerly, one country sending its produce to another country, or one nation sending its raw material to another nation, we shall be in the way of having whole continents engaged in raising the raw material required for the manufacturing communities of another hemisphere. It is our interest to prevent, as far as possible, the sudden interruption of such a state of dependence; and, therefore, I would suggest it as a most desirable thing to be done in all cases by our Government, as the ruling and guiding principle of their policy, that they should seek in their negotiations of treaties to bind the parties respectively, not, as a belligerent act, to prevent the exportation of anything, unless we except certain munitions of war, or armaments. I don't think the Government should interfere to prevent the merchant from exporting any article, *even if it can be made available for warlike purposes. The Government has nothing to do with mercantile operations; it ought not to undertake the surveillance of commerce at all. Of course it should not allow an enemy to come here and fit out ships or armaments to be used in fighting against us.* But I mean, that for all articles of legitimate commerce, there ought to be, as far as possible, freedom in time of war. To what I am urging it may be said, 'But you won't get people to observe these international obligations, even if they are entered into.' That remark was made in

[1] *Speeches on Questions of Public Policy by Richard Cobden, M.P.*, Vol. II. p. 298. (London: Macmillan, 1870.)

the House of Commons by a Minister, who, I think, ought not to have uttered such a prediction. *Why are any international obligations undertaken unless they are to be observed?* We have this guarantee, that the international rules I am now advocating will be respected; that they are not contemplated to be merely an article in a Treaty between any two Powers, but to be fundamental laws regulating the intercourse of nations, and having the assent of the majority of, if not all, the maritime Powers in the world. Let us suppose two countries to be at war, and that one of them has entered into an engagement not to stop the exportation of grain. Well, we will assume the temptation to be so great, that, thinking it can starve its cpponent, it would wish to stop this exportation in spite of the Treaty. Why, that would bring down on them instantly the animosity, indeed the hostility, of all the other Powers who were parties to the system. *The nation which has been a party to a general system of international law becomes an outlaw to all nations if it breaks its engagement towards any one.* And in the case on which I am laying great stress—viz. that of commercial blockade, and the prevention of any stoppage of exports in time of war—I don't rely on the honour of the individual nation making it for observing the law; I rely on its being her interest to keep it, because if she were at war with us, and were to break the law, she would not break it as against us alone, but as against the whole world."[1]

[1] Italics inserted.

# APPENDIX II

The following extract from the Report of the Machinery of Government Committee of the Ministry of Reconstruction, referred to above,[1] is interesting as showing that the problem of the relationship between the Government Departments and Parliament was already exciting attention, even before the international extension of the Departments, through the working of the League of Nations, had taken place:

### Parliamentary Control

"48. We cannot conclude this Part of our Report without a reference to the bearing of our inquiry upon the problem of Parliamentary Control. Our terms of reference direct us to frame our recommendations with the primary object of promoting the efficient and economical working of the public service. But we have throughout our deliberations borne in mind the fact that any action directed to this end would fail to achieve its purpose if it were to have the effect of disturbing the balance of authority between the Legislature and the Executive.

"It would, we think, be generally felt that any improvement in the organization of the Departments of State which was so marked as substantially to increase their efficiency should have as its correlative an increase in the power of the Legislature as the check upon the acts and proposals of the Executive.

"49. We need scarcely say that we adhere without reserve to this view. But our duty is limited to the consideration of the present defects of departmental organisation and the suggestion of appropriate remedies. It is for Parliament to see that its own supremacy is not impaired. . . .

"52. We should hesitate to enter further upon questions of procedure which Parliament alone can examine or determine with authority, were it not that it has been definitely suggested to us that the efficiency of the public service would be improved if steps

[1]See p. 19.

were taken to secure the continuous and well-informed interest of a Parliamentary body in the execution by each Department of the policy which Parliament has laid down.

"53. It has been suggested that the appointment of a series of Standing Committees, each charged with the consideration of the activities of the Departments which cover the main divisions of the business of Government, would be conducive to this end. Any such Committees would require to be furnished with full information as to the course of administration pursued by the Departments with which they were concerned; and for this purpose it would be requisite that Ministers, as well as the officers of Departments, should appear before them to explain and defend the acts for which they were responsible.

"54. It is not for us to attempt to forecast the precise procedure under which interrogations and requests for papers emanating from such Committees should be dealt with. But the particular argument in favour of some such system to which we feel justified in drawing attention is that if Parliament were furnished, through such Committees of its members, with fuller knowledge of the work of Departments, and of the objects which Ministers had in view, the officers of Departments would be encouraged to lay more stress upon constructive work in administering the services entrusted to them for the benefit of the community than upon anticipating criticism which may, in present conditions, often be based upon imperfect knowledge of the facts or the principles at issue."[1]

Distinct from this problem of the relation of individual Departments to Parliament, but closely related to it, is the problem of establishing some organized relationship between the international affairs, or the domestic affairs with international repercussions, of the various Departments themselves. This is, in essence the problem brought to light in Berlin by Mr. Parker Gilbert's Memorandum, and it has been dealt with, at least partially, in Germany by the device of a standing Interdepartmental Committee. The position of Mr. Gilbert himself as a sort of

[1]British Parliamentary Paper, *Cmd*. 9230, 1918, pp. 14-15. (H.M. Stationery Office. *6d*.)

recognized observer from the outside world, with the right to bring his views to the attention of the Government before contemplated policies have assumed public shape, is one that invites reflection.

# DATE DUE

| | | | |
|---|---|---|---|
| | | | |
| | | | |
| | | | |
| | | | |
| | | | |
| | | | |
| | | | |
| | | | |
| | | | |
| | | | |
| | | | |

GAYLORD                  PRINTED IN U.S.A.